Praise for Stabbed  in the

"I'm a doctor who tr[...] and lasting pain of sudden, [...] book helps me. It can help you. Two remarkable women have woven their singular life stories together, describing the murders of their children, their own sense of shock, betrayal and despair, and then the ways they found sustenance and support, hope and love, and, ultimately, the energy and will to reform institutions and to assist others. We owe Lynn and Nancy more than recognition and gratitude. We owe them the brief time it takes to read their accounts, to absorb their skills in coping with cruelty, and to carry on their mission of embracing and encouraging those who suffer the most severe of human wounds."
⌒Frank M. Ochberg, MD, a pioneer in the study of trauma, Clinical Professor of Psychiatry, Michigan State University

"In this deeply moving book, two mothers share their personal stories of incredible grief and loss but also transcendence. They also share invaluable reflections and suggestions. This combination of testimony and reflection makes it essential reading for anyone who has lost a loved one to murder, or who is walking with someone who has, or who wants to understand the journey better—and for reporters who cover the crime beat."
⌒Howard Zehr, Distinguished Professor of Restorative Justice and author of *Transcending: Reflections of Crime Victims* and *The Little Book of Restorative Justice*

"In life, as in sports, it takes courage and resilience to carry on in the face of adversity. The two mothers in this deeply moving book demonstrate these qualities each and every day. Their lives, and this book, are inspirational and a living testament of the power of the human spirit."
⌒Dennis "Denny" Green, one of the most successful coaches in NFL history

"Two mothers take you by the hand and walk you through their worst nightmare to illustrate the gut-wrenching effects of the murders of their children. Their stories will educate you about how, individually, they have advocated for and made changes to the systems that failed them. *Stabbed in the Heart* illustrates how the most harmed in our society are often the only ones who can bring about effective change."

⁓Jennifer Storm, author of *Blackout Girl, Leave the Light On* and *Picking Up the Pieces Without Picking Up*

"*Stabbed in the Heart* provides a graphic insight into the deepest of assaults to the human spirit. It is also an incredible story of struggle, resilience, and hope. Lynn and Nancy have written a book that provides a comprehensive perspective for both layman and therapist."

⁓Jeff Verrecchio, Psychologist

"*Stabbed in the Heart* is the powerful, honest story of two mothers who survived the unthinkable, learned how to live again and use their experience to help others. It gives practical advice on how to cope with the devastating consequences of homicide. I recommend this book to families of homicide victims and anyone who cares about them—read this book and you will understand."

⁓Kathleen O'Hara, MA, author of *A Grief Like No Other, surviving the violent death of someone you love*

Stabbed in the Heart

To Penny,
Peace and blessings!
bright Shine

Nancy Eshelman

love, life
and Happiness

Best of 2014,
Nancy Eshelman

Stabbed in the Heart

Three Murdered Children

Two Resilient Mothers

Lynn Shiner & Nancy Chavez

with Nancy Eshelman

RJD Blessings, LLC

STABBED IN THE HEART

Book cover and interior design by Sarah E. Holroyd (http://sleepingcatbooks.com)

ISBN-13: 978-0-9898717-0-9

Library of Congress Control Number: 2013916953

First printing 2013. Printed in the United States of America

10 9 8 7 6 5 4 3 2 1

Please contact the publisher at the address below to order additional copies or obtain information about bulk discount pricing:

Order Dept.
RJD Blessings
P.O. Box 61431
Harrisburg, PA 17106-1431

Or visit our website: www.RJDBlessings.com

We dedicate this book in memory of our precious children:

Randi, Jen & Dave

Acknowledgments

I t is our hope that, in some small way, the words printed on these pages will help others understand the impact of crime and the important role of family, friends and community.

There are so many people who helped bring this book to life. Most importantly, we are grateful to two very special people in our lives, Greg Green and Paul Shiner, for being fabulous sounding boards, as well incredibly generous with their encouragement, insight, critique, unconditional love and support throughout this process.

Our sincere appreciation goes to Nancy Eshelman for her patience and insightful questions to capture our voices and help write our story with clarity. She is a gifted listener and was able to bring the countless interviews to life for our readers. We had a common belief that this book wasn't only for victims of crime but could impact any reader who consumed its contents.

We are indebted to our family members, friends and the professionals whose perspectives helped to confirm the facts in this book, provide insight to various chapters or were willing to share how Randi, Jen or David's deaths continue to impact their lives. A special thanks to Father Snyder, Pastor Wirick, Jeff Verrecchio, Samantha Krepps, Linda Morrison, Alison (Delsite) Everett, Judy Yupcavage, Carol Lavery, Kathy Buckley, Mary Achilles, David Freed, Ed Marsico, Gabriella Camplese, Steve Marquart, Heidi Klimpke, Jill Berry, Linda Wilson, Michael Wilson, Brenda Gould, Emily Pearson, Karen Lilley, Lara Young, Deb Donahue, Deb Salas, Ed Monk, Ed Katz, Shannon Wood, Kathy Wilson, and Leo and Ruthie Brown.

We are also indebted to Diane Miller for her keen editorial skills and delivering the title of our book and to Todd Shill, Sarah Holroyd, Jennifer Storm and Phyllis Parsons for professional advice.

Murray, Lynn's cat, who brought her much comfort and was always looking for a lap or a pile of papers to sprawl out on, received some of the best rubbings of his life during this project.

Special thanks to all of the victims of crime who have shared their heartfelt pain. Thank you for being a source of courage, strength, inspiration and knowledge.

We have been blessed with family, friends, colleagues and professionals who have loved, supported, guided and traveled with us since the deaths of Randi, Jen and Dave. Our communities have been extremely supportive as our journeys unfolded, leaving us with hope that something good can come out of our personal tragedies.

Contents

Foreword

I have been a fan of crime stories for many years. Most have the same format: a ghastly murder, a police investigation and a trial. The end.

When Lynn Shiner and Nancy Chavez contacted me about writing this book, they suggested something very different: a book about what happens in the aftermath, when everyone has gone home. How do two women, two mothers, go on after the loss of their only children? How do they get up every morning and put one foot in front of the other? What motivates them? What matters to them? How can they possibly continue living their lives?

I knew who Lynn and Nancy were before our first meeting. Twenty-four years working at the local newspaper makes you familiar with a lot of people you might never really know. Like thousands of others, I had read about them, and their murdered children, in the newspaper. Like others, I had shivered in horror.

Later, I had met Lynn casually, maybe once or twice. I met Nancy at a dinner party. I admired them in the way I admire all strong women. Once we launched this project, my admiration grew. The three of us sat for hours, sometimes as a trio, other times in a pair. They poured out their hearts and relived their emotions. They shared stories of friends and acquaintances who said the right thing, and those whose words were very wrong. They talked about the media, the clergy, and how their words impacted their lives. They talked about the stages of grief and how they manifested themselves. They talked about forgiveness and whether it is truly possible for the mother of a murdered child to forgive. At times, we laughed together; other times we cried. I met and interviewed their friends, members of their families, Nancy's priest, Lynn's pastor and psychologist, and a district attorney.

I came to realize that what they had endured, losing their only children to murder, was almost beyond comprehension. How does a mother come back from that? Where does she find the inner strength to go on? For both of them, the answer seems to be in a cause. In caring for others, fighting injustice, they have given their lives new meaning. They will never forget their children or their horrible losses, but through their efforts, they have found a way to honor David, Jennifer and Randi.

I think they were drawn to me, in part, because I had recently lost my grown son to cancer. I had shared his last months with the readers of my weekly column in The Patriot-News. Writing the story of Bill's final journey helped me deal with the experience of losing a child, and brought love and support from unexpected places.

What Lynn and Nancy didn't know when we started was that murder also had touched my life in an ugly and horrifying way. The murder happened in 1979 in Lancaster, a city about 40 miles from Harrisburg where I live now. When I changed jobs in 1985 and moved here, I tried to leave the murder behind. Perhaps my co-workers knew about it; we did, after all, work for a newspaper. But I never discussed it with them or with any of the friends I made. It was as if I had packed the baggage away and left it behind. Or so I thought. The time I spent sharing honest, open emotions with Lynn and Nancy made me realize that while I hadn't shared the story, I still was carrying much of the baggage.

Lynn and Nancy both experienced abuse in their marriages. So did I. My husband, the father of my two sons, could be physically abusive. But the emotional abuse was constant. I was stupid. I was fat, homely. I wasn't a good wife or mother. If I talked to any man, any place, any time, I must be cheating.

Somewhere, somehow, I found the gumption to plot my escape. I started college, determined to earn a degree, begin a career, gather my boys, and leave. I wanted to do it before he ruined them, too.

In October 1978, we left him. I had a job, an apartment and not much else. But I didn't care; I was free – or so I thought. He hounded me, hassled me and made it a point to know my whereabouts. That was before anyone used the word "stalking," but stalking was exactly what he did. He used my children as an excuse to know where I was and what I was doing. He used them as an excuse to show up at my front door any time of the day or night. One evening after my boys and I were settled, he shoved his way into my apartment, ripped my telephone out of the wall, and pushed me down a flight of stairs.

To understand why I didn't call the police, you have to understand the times. There was no 911, no protection from abuse or domestic violence shelters. People didn't talk much about those kinds of things then. Even my Mother suggested these things wouldn't have happened if I'd just been nicer.

One night in February 1979, a co-worker stopped by my apartment unexpectedly. He'd been there before, and I invited him in and we watched TV while my boys slept. Neither of us knew that my estranged husband had climbed the trellis outside my window and seen us watching television, then driven home, and gotten a gun. When he returned, he shattered the front window, stormed into my apartment and – with his own children sleeping in the next room -- shot my friend dead.

There were no victim advocates in 1979. No one took my children and me under their wing. Just days after the murder, my best friend and I, on our hands and knees, scrubbed blood and bits of flesh from the walls of my apartment. I couldn't live there. With my husband, unbelievably, out on bail, I cowered in my new apartment. Eventually, the boys and I moved in with my friend and her two children. I was terrified to be alone.

Meanwhile, my husband's parents hired a top-notch defense lawyer who convinced a jury that my husband was just a poor guy trying to keep his family together while his wicked wife educated herself and left him in the dust. The jury bought it, and he served only five years in prison. When he was released, he walked the streets as though nothing had happened. My sense of dread finally disappeared when, a few years later, he died after a truck hit him while he was crossing a street.

Many of those feelings bubbled to the surface in the months I sat with Nancy and Lynn. I felt their rage, their powerlessness. I understood when they talked about friends who deserted them and family who wanted talk of the murders to go away. I can't begin to understand their loss of their children in such violence, but I do share some of their emotions. And, eventually, I shared my story with them.

This book is their story, not mine, but Lynn felt strongly that I should share with you, the reader, what happened to me. We find it ironic, and perhaps appropriate, that they chose me to write this book. I am honored. The more time I spend with Lynn and Nancy, the more I appreciate the human spirit. If these women were able to climb out of the depths of depression that followed their loss, then the rest of us can survive anything. They are strong women whom I admire even more now.

Neither woman wants to dwell on the acts that led to the loss of their children. We share the stories of the murders not to relive them, but to help readers understand the terror and pain these women endured.

Lynn's horror, and her journey back, began on Christmas day 1994. Nancy lost her beloved Randi more than eight years later, on Jan. 10, 2003. As you will discover when you read their words, people heal at their own pace and in their own way. If Lynn and Nancy seem to be at different places in their journeys, it is for two reasons: They are different people, and Lynn began walking her path years before Nancy.

This book tells their stories. They have chosen to share them to do what both of them do so well – help others. Perhaps in reading these pages, someone who has experienced loss will find reassurance. Perhaps their stories can offer lessons to the families, friends and acquaintances of those who have faced horror in their lives.

Perhaps, they hope, someone may see in the stories of their lives a nugget of evidence, a hint of the sinister – and it will prevent another tragedy.

Nancy Eshelman
November 2013

Chapter 1

Lynn Shares Her Black Christmas

Christmas 1994 dawned as an unseasonably warm day in Harrisburg, Pennsylvania. All I needed to start the celebration was my children.

In those first early hours, I was anticipating the wide smile on David's face when he saw his new mountain bike. I envisioned Jen gushing and fawning over her wonderful new clothes.

That would be the last pleasant memory I had for a long time.

Jennifer, 10, and David, 8, had spent the night with their father, Tom Snead, my ex-husband. According to our custody agreement, it was Tom's turn to have the children overnight Christmas Eve into Christmas morning.

I had called Tom's house the first thing that morning, hoping I could pick up the children early. We had planned to go to my parents' home to spend the day with my boyfriend, Paul Shiner, and my large extended family. I thought it odd when no one answered, and wondered if Tom had taken the children out to breakfast or outside to try out a new toy.

Around 8:30, I decided to drive to Tom's house. As I hopped on Interstate 81, I felt my stomach knot in anticipation that something was not right. I told myself that I was overreacting and I dismissed my gloomy thoughts as I turned into Tom's development.

His car was in the driveway and the Christmas lights were on, but no one answered when I knocked. I knocked louder. Then I tried the door and found it unlocked. I opened the door about six inches, and paused for several seconds.

Normally, I would have walked in, but something stopped me that morning. Instead, I shut the door and knocked again. Eventually, I gave up and drove home.

The knot in my stomach tightened. "Wait," I told myself, "you weren't supposed to pick them up until 10 a.m. They have gone to a neighbor's, or someone picked them up and they all went out for breakfast."

When I arrived home, I called repeatedly. No one answered. When Paul arrived at 10 a.m., we unloaded the kids' presents we had hidden at his home and drove together to Tom's. Once again, no one answered the door.

I walked around the house, peered in the sliding glass door and saw Tom on the couch. How could he be sleeping so late on Christmas morning with children in the house? Surely Jennifer and David would have awakened early in search of Santa's gifts.

Then, to my horror, I saw blood. Awash in panic, I was frozen to the spot and called for Paul. After he looked through the glass door and saw the blood staining the white couch and the front of Tom's clothes, Paul yelled to a neighbor who had been washing his car to call 911.

The neighbor assumed that I was the one who needed assistance, since my legs felt like rubber and I was having difficulty walking across the street. Paul led me to the curb and sat down with me until the neighbor connected with 911. After the call, Paul told the neighbor what he saw through the sliding glass door and asked him to go in the house with him to look for the children. The two men, strangers to one another, walked into a nightmare.

In a house decorated for Christmas, they found Tom dead on the living room couch, a knife at the end of his fingers. Paul and the neighbor ran up the stairs looking for the children. Paul told me later that with each step, he prayed that the children weren't there. The faster he moved, the more it seemed everything happened in slow motion. As he approached the top of the stairs, his legs felt like lead weights, making it difficult for him to walk.

Paul looked to his right and saw twin beds. On the bed farthest from him, he saw David, partially covered by sheets. Paul and the neighbor could see a significant amount of blood throughout the room. Even from 10 feet away, Paul knew that David was dead.

Paul told the neighbor they needed to look for Jennifer. They walked down the hall to the other bedroom, where bunk beds filled one corner. Jennifer was nestled in the lower bed with the covers drawn up to her neck. Next to her was a bunny I had bought for her when she was born.

Paul knew it was too late for Jen, too, but he felt compelled to extend his hand and touch her cold face.

After an unsteady trip down the stairs, Paul paused for several seconds in the living room. The lighted Christmas tree in the corner of the room caught his eye. There were no presents under the tree. He looked from the tree to Tom's body, unable to believe what was happening. There was only one word exploding in his mind -- why? As he walked out of the house, Paul felt as if he were watching somebody else in a movie. Each step increased his sense of dread. He was going to have to tell me that my children were dead.

I was sitting on the curb rocking, the neighbor's wife beside me. When I looked up and saw Paul, absolutely white, I knew. Over and over, I asked him if the kids were OK. I begged him to tell me that the kids were not there.

Paul wouldn't answer. He didn't have to. His face spoke volumes.

"They're dead, aren't they?" I repeated again and again. After about the third time, he whispered, "Yes, they are." I fell to my knees and began vomiting in the street. When I got up, I started to move toward the house. I wanted to see my babies.

But Paul and the neighbor held me back as I screamed for Jen and Dave.

When Paul and I try to remember that horrific day, we see snippets. Details remain fuzzy. I remember Paul and the neighbor helping me into his house. I recall being in the kitchen, where dinner preparations had abruptly stopped.

I paced among the kitchen, living room and bathroom. I remember sitting on a couch, tugging at my arms, wringing my hands. My hands seemed uncontrollable; they traveled from my feet to my knees to my legs. They clutched at my heart, touched my neck, face and head. I remember feeling ill.

Paul, a pharmacist, remembers feeling concern for my well-being. My heart was racing, I was pale, I couldn't talk and my blood pressure had dropped. Paul was frightened by how unstable I was. Someone called the paramedics and a crisis intervention team, and Paul called the family doctor to try to get something to stop the shaking and slow my heart rate.

I wanted someone to call my parents, but at the same time I feared what this news would do to them. At their home in nearby Perry County, my parents and other family members wondered what was keeping us. My dad, Ed Monk, tried calling my house. When he got no answer, he would wait a few minutes and try again.

Finally, his phone rang. Paul told him there had been an accident and he should come immediately.

My Dad wanted to know if everyone was OK. Paul told him I was. Then he struggled to get the words out.

"Ed," Paul said, "Tom killed the kids. You've got to come down here."

When my father and brother-in-law arrived, they were overwhelmed by the activity and sheer number of vehicles. The street was filled with police cars, an ambulance, vehicles from TV stations and the coroner's van.

Paul left me in the care of the neighbors and went outside to tell my father and brother-in-law what he knew. An officer tried to talk with me, but I was incoherent. One of the men asked police if we could leave. He was told we could, after we provided an address and phone number where we could be reached and agreed not to leave the area.

We drove away, leaving my children behind.

Police were just beginning to string crime scene tape around the property. Detectives and officers still had to process the crime scene, take photographs and measurements, interview neighbors and collect and bag evidence. The medical examiner would have to rule officially what we already knew – my children were dead.

Paul and I cannot remember who drove, but somehow we made it back to my house. Through my searing pain, I worried about the desserts I had made for the family Christmas gathering. I insisted on taking them to my parents' house.

I remember listening to the messages on my voice mail. Most were from media wanting to talk with me. I paced back and forth from Jen's bedroom to Dave's, shaking my head and squeezing my hands together, thinking what had happened just couldn't be real. I knew in my heart I was not going to make it through the days ahead.

As I wandered through my house, I picked up all the photo albums I could find. My brother-in-law, who had been instructed not to let me out of his sight for even a minute, followed my every step. Paul went next door to share the horrific news with Scott and Lisa Hartranft, who, along with their children, had been very close to the children and me.

When we arrived in Perry County, Paul walked me up the sidewalk of my parents' home. I wasn't talking or crying. Like a zombie, I simply did what I was told. The front door opened, and my mother was standing there with her arms stretched out. That's when the tears flowed. "Mom," I wailed, "I don't have my babies anymore."

From then on, the tears didn't stop. I spent Christmas Day with my family, a bottle of Valium and a pair of scissors, cutting Tom out of every family photo.

Back at Tom's house, police called in Ed Marsico, 31, an assistant district attorney in Dauphin County whose wife was pregnant with their first child. Ed had volunteered to be on call because his extended family lived in the county. Taking the on-call duty would free others in his office to spend Christmas with out-of-town family.

Volunteering for duty took him from his family celebration to the home of Tom Snead. There, police filled in the horrible details.

As midnight ushered in Christmas, Tom had walked into his daughter Jennifer's bedroom and stabbed her one time in the heart with a six-inch steak knife from the kitchen. No one will ever know if David was awake from the anticipation of Christmas or if his sister screamed and woke him. What investigators do know is that David got out of bed and started walking towards his father.

As David went into his arms, Tom stabbed him four times in the upper and lower back. David struggled. He fought for his life. He tried to grab the knife, the same knife Tom had used to stab Jennifer. Investigators know this because they saw the cuts on his hands. Hair in the cuts offered evidence that David had grabbed his father's hair as he struggled to pull free. His father stabbed him four more times in the chest and stomach, then carried David to his bed and tucked him in.

The police estimate that Tom killed himself two to four hours later. He cleaned himself up and cleaned the knife he used to murder his children. He placed the knife on the bottom shelf of the end table next to the couch. He left a Bible on the coffee table. Then he stuck a three-inch paring knife into his own heart. Written on his sweater vest and his right thigh in black ink were the words "King of kings, Lord of lords."

Investigators surmised that Tom thought he was God. They determined he had been planning this ending for a year. He had written a checklist. The last item was "Kill Jennifer and David."

Ed carries two vivid images from that day. A group of cops, surveying the carnage, lamented Tom Snead's death. They would have preferred to finish the job themselves.

The other image was a plate of cookies and a plastic bag full of miniature carrots prepared for Santa's arrival. "The kids had written notes to Santa Claus," Ed said. "That just really got to me. That's the one thing I will never forget from that scene."

In the days after Jennifer and David died, I learned there had been signs that Tom's sense of reality had been dwindling. He had been stalking a female disc jockey, had smashed the windshield of her car and left her a note on the back of a bank receipt, saying, "You're nothing but a Liar, Drop Dead!" For those acts, he had been arrested in November and faced a trial in the coming months.

Tom's odd and threatening behavior compelled the disc jockey to call the state police and express her fears for my children. Tom, she said, had used Jennifer to call in dedications to the radio station. He wanted her to play mean break-up songs dedicated to certain women.

There I was with primary custody, and no one had told me any of this. I didn't know about the phone call to the state police, the radio requests by Jennifer or Tom's arrest for stalking and harassment.

Why didn't I know?

As the weeks unfolded, I learned there was more that I didn't know. Tom, claiming he was part of Epiphany Lutheran Church's outreach ministry, had visited patients at Lancaster General Hospital, frightening them with his bizarre beliefs. He had told a co-worker of mine that he was taking our children to see God. He had asked friends if they would consider adopting Jen and Dave. When another co-worker inquired about his well-being, he responded that life on earth was going to get really bad and then it would change and be beautiful and peaceful.

In November, Tom had told me he had met a woman in Canada, a rich, famous woman, and he might be marrying her soon. After the children died, I learned that his fantasy love was singer Celine Dion.

I always knew, as many others did, that Tom was odd. He had trouble expressing feelings and had a very bad temper. He told me he had attempted suicide as a teenager because the parents of his girlfriend forbade him to see her. (She later became his first wife.) He drank three or four pots of coffee a day and apparently heard voices. He refused to seek any type of counseling or take medications. He blamed all of his problems on other people. Nothing was ever Tom's fault.

Each of these pieces was a part of the puzzle that was Tom. A variety of people held those pieces. What everyone lacked who knew Tom, including me, were enough pieces to put the puzzle together. Alone, each piece made Tom seem a bit strange. If he had sought professional help, a psychiatrist or psychologist might have put them together and realized Tom was a ticking time bomb.

No one, including me, imagined he would harm our children. Even though I had experienced many acts of strange behavior, weird comments and emotional and physical abuse during our relationship, I still encouraged the children's relationship with their father. I never wanted my kids to hate him, and they wanted their father in their lives, even though he constantly broke promises he made to them. None of us realized that his strange behavior throughout his life indicated severe mental health issues.

Now I had to do what no parent should ever have to do: bury my beautiful children.

I vaguely remember going to the funeral home and being shown child-sized caskets. I kept shaking my head, telling them that Jen and Dave couldn't be buried in those. The people at the funeral home explained that state law required the children to be in caskets. If I didn't like a certain casket, there were others to choose from. But I kept saying no and began to have a panic attack. Once I calmed down, I told them Jen and Dave could not be alone. They needed to be together.

Finally, with help, I chose an adult casket that allowed each child's head to be placed at an end with their legs touching in the center. I had decided that the casket would not be open. I just couldn't bear the thought of seeing my precious children dead. My oldest brother, Gene, stepped in and said, "Sis, I'm not going to let you do that. You, along with many others, need to see Jen and Dave. We will be there with you. I need you to listen to me." So, I did.

Most of the other decisions about the funeral, burial and reception were left to my family, who stepped up and handled all the details. For that, I was grateful.

But to this day I swear the toughest and most painful, heart-wrenching thing I've ever had to do was to see Jen and Dave's cold and still faces.

To steel myself for the funeral, I spent the morning swallowing Valium, seven pills in all, in a futile attempt to stop my heart from racing and ease my uncontrollable shaking. I knew what had happened, but seeing my children's bodies was about to make it real. When we got to the funeral home, I entered the main door but wouldn't budge from the outer room. I stood firm and shook my head no. I wasn't ready. I could hear the sobbing and wailing as my parents, siblings and nieces and nephews saw Jen and Dave.

Paul was by my side, telling me I needed to go to the casket. Walking through the funeral home to view them took all the courage I could muster. I went reluctantly, feeling as if I were in someone else's body.

There was my beautiful Jen, wearing her favorite dress. David, ever the boy, wore his favorite attire too, jeans and a rugby shirt. The two of them were surrounded by things that were precious to them: a doll baby and afghan made by their grandmother, pictures of family and friends, a Cabbage Patch kid, a remote control car, Matchbox cars, baseball cards, unopened Christmas presents, jewelry, books and notes written to them from several people who attended their viewing. I laid my head on their chests. My tears soaked their clothing. I couldn't stop touching them, fondling their hair and smoothing their clothing. I needed to see the cuts on David's hand that proved how he had fought for his life. In death, my little boy looked angry, while Jen's face carried a peaceful expression.

I went through the motions, hugged and cried with hundreds of mourners and showed as many people as could bear to look at the cuts in David's little hands.

To this day, I can't fully explain the depth of my sadness, emptiness and fear. Your children aren't allowed to die before you.

In the days and weeks that followed, I really knew what it meant to have a broken heart. I felt like I had a 50-pound block on my chest. My family wouldn't let me out of their sight for a single second, as there was nothing behind my eyes except a pool of blackness and a sense that I was considering ending my life. They were right.

Chapter 2

Looking Back

The story of my relationship with Tom begins with my move to the city. I was just 18, had graduated in a class of 80 and had landed a job in Harrisburg, working for the state. I left home with a real sense of excitement, anticipating that working in the state capital would be exciting. I envisioned friendly co-workers, parties and paychecks.

I was a naïve girl, an introvert who had grown up in a rural area, a bit of a tomboy who owned a dirt bike and hunted. I was very shy and the baby of our family. My mother used to introduce me as the "accident." Growing up, I was chubby, although my mother described me as "big boned." My siblings always claimed I was spoiled and got away with a lot more than they ever had. Frankly, they were right.

While I grew up with this wonderful, loving mother and a father who worked extremely hard to provide for his family, in my teen years I suffered from low self-esteem. I had some great friends, but I thought they outpaced me. They were pretty, thin, engaging and popular. Boys liked them.

My grades were A's and B's. I played field hockey and was picked for the all-star team. I was a cheerleader and captain of the squad. Truth be told, I hated everything about cheering, but I stuck it out because I desperately wanted to fit in.

By the time I turned 17, all my friends talked about was boyfriends and sex. It seemed they all had been or were in sexual relationships. Once again, I was the outcast. Then, the summer before my senior year, feeling peer pressure, I had the opportunity to fit in. I went with a bunch of girls and their families to the Poconos. I lost my virginity to a boy at Lake Wallenpaupak. I had met him only two days before and never saw him again. It was a dreadful experience, but now, at least, I could brag and share details with my friends. I simply wanted what all teenage girls want, to be liked and accepted.

A couple of months later, I agreed to go to a stranger's house with a friend who was planning to spend time there with her boyfriend. I had seen the man who lived there but had never spoken to him. He was in his early 30s. I sat on the couch, not saying anything, until someone handed me a drink. The next thing I remember is waking up in a bed, naked, scared and disoriented. I had been drugged and raped.

I didn't understand why I felt as though I was drunk. But I felt alone, ashamed and guilty, and I blamed myself. First, I had lied to my parents about where I was going, and second, I should never have gone to someone's house that I barely knew. I didn't tell the friends that I was with what had happened. I told no one. It was humiliating.

I remember getting home after midnight, past curfew, and lying to my parents that I ran out of gas. All I wanted to do was take a shower, but I knew that would raise too many questions. So I simply crawled into bed feeling dirty and used and questioned myself over and over why I let this happen.

After that, I was gripped with fear. I was quieter than normal, and I just wanted to stay in my house close to my Mom. I didn't feel safe, and I can remember many times being afraid at night and standing by my mother's bedside. Instinctively, she knew I was there. She wouldn't say a word. She would just move over and allow me to crawl in beside her.

As an adult, looking back, I think I reacted the way many girls would. I tried to forget the whole thing and pretend it had never happened. Call the police? Not even a thought. It was simply all my fault, and why would I ever want anyone to know?

Weeks later, I saw the person in a place a group of us often hung out, and I could feel my body become tense. He had the nerve to walk right over to me, acting like we were now friends who had shared a good time.

My self-esteem, never high to begin with, plummeted more. I was at the age of partying and took that term to an all-new level. Over the next couple of years, I didn't simply drink to socialize. I drank to erase the feelings of disgust, disappointment and depression. I was out of control and began a period of heavy weekend drinking and promiscuity. The alcohol numbed my pain and having sex confirmed that men liked me. I tried to be in relationships, but they didn't last because I had very little self-worth and was always looking for reasons why it wouldn't work.

Several months after being raped, I was driving the back roads with a friend, sharing a bottle of Jack Daniels. I know it was wrong, but it was the 1970s. Drinking and driving was common, and the thought that anyone would be hurt by my actions never crossed my mind.

I lost control of the car going around a curve, went over an embankment and hit head-on a tree that was almost as big as the Volkswagen Beetle I was driving. There was a lot of blood. We were able to crawl out of the car and up the embankment and walk about a quarter-mile to the nearest house, where they called an ambulance. We were both severely bruised. My friend had a broken nose, and I can remember being on the operating table with the plastic surgeon sewing 110 stitches to reconnect my eyebrow and fix a cut in my forehead. All the while the surgeon was singing, "In heaven there is no beer."

Three months later, I headed to Harrisburg, where I met Tom. He was 30, the divorced father of two, and worked in the same bureau. We became friends. I wasn't used to someone like Tom. He seemed to like me, wanted to get to know me, wanted to know my thoughts. He would offer compliments, buy me coffee or soda at break time, and treat me to dinner at Bob's Big Boy. He seemed nice and kind and generous, but I didn't feel an attraction to him. Still, I figured with my background and all the things I had done, perhaps Tom was the best I could hope for. Within a year, a more serious relationship had developed, but it didn't take me long to realize the relationship was not on solid ground. I was too young, we had almost nothing in common, he was talking marriage and kids, and I was thinking there was nothing right about this relationship.

The more I backed away, the harder Tom pushed. It was as if he heard nothing I said. He wanted to be part of my life, period. After I told Tom I didn't want to see him anymore, he would follow me home from work and sit in his car in the parking lot of my apartment complex. He was stalking me, but at the time, it wasn't a crime. He called constantly, telling me he couldn't live without me and would do anything to get me back. He demanded to know why I was doing this to him.

Tom's moods shifted from helpless to angry and back. He would lose his temper, then apologize with gifts, constantly pushing me for a fresh start. I wasn't interested.

After about four weeks, a fire in Tom's apartment building left him with almost no possessions and nowhere to stay. He asked to stay temporarily with my roommate and me. I felt sorry for him and agreed. When my roommate decided to enlist in the reserves, Tom offered to stay for 12 weeks to cover her share of the bills while she was at training. The 12 weeks turned into a year, and then two. During this time, Tom encouraged me to spend money and extend my credit. Soon I was financially dependent on him.

But Tom and I weren't getting along. In the summer of 1983, with financial help from my roommate, I asked Tom to leave. In August, I discovered I was pregnant.

Tom wanted to marry me, and I felt I had no choice. At 22, I felt unable to handle life as a single parent. I considered abortion, but knew it wasn't the right choice for me. And I could hear the infamous words of my dad, "You made your bed, now lie in it."

Tom and I attended marital preparation classes. When we were finished, the pastor advised me not to marry Tom. But the wedding went on. I stood at the altar and prayed that someone would speak up when the pastor said, "If anyone sees any reason why this couple should not be wed in holy matrimony, speak now or forever hold your peace." No one spoke, because no one knew how wrong this was but me.

The mental abuse began soon after we said "I do." I was 125 pounds, but Tom called me fat. He told me I was ugly and should be grateful to him for marrying me. He demanded to know the "real" father of our child. For the first year or two, the abuse was only verbal. He had such anger and hatred towards me that at times I actually wished that he would just hit me and get it over with.

I never knew when his mood would change or what vile and hateful words would spew in my direction.

The first year of our marriage, we rented an apartment four doors from Tom's brother and his wife. I thought it was great to have family close by. For whatever reason, he was jealous and resentful of his brother and insisted that I not visit them unless he was present.

Meanwhile, he constantly put me down, told me I was disgusting to look at during my pregnancy, made mooing sounds when I walked by him and refused to have intercourse with me for the first year of our marriage. I soon learned that he preferred masturbation with porn videos and magazines to me.

I repeatedly found oil missing from the kitchen and a hardened cloth under the sofa -- leaving me feeling disgusted, angry and hurt. But as time progressed, I began to feel relieved that he was obsessed with porn and masturbation. It meant he would leave me alone.

But Tom's abuse eventually escalated to the physical with a shove, a push, hair pulling. Like many abused women, I felt isolated and blamed myself for provoking Tom. I reasoned if

I could hold on a little longer, Jen would be older and I could take her and leave. And then I was pregnant with David.

To outsiders, we might have appeared to be the perfect family: attractive mother, prosperous father, two beautiful blond, blue-eyed children, a girl and a boy. But Tom marched to his own tune and refused to be a part of a family. We rarely did anything together, unless family wanted to visit. Then he acted the role of the "good family man." If we had plans to visit my family, he would always say he wasn't going at the last minute, and I would be so disappointed and actually beg him to go. It was important to me that he be a part of my family. Sometimes my begging worked. Sometimes I had to make up excuses for his absences. He preferred to stay downstairs in his office until 4 or 5 a.m. watching television, and then sleep until noon or 1 p.m. He wanted his meals cooked but didn't eat with us. Unless I constantly nagged, he wasn't helpful with the kids, chores or yard work. After a while, I just stopped asking and tried to do most of it by myself, and as the kids got older, they became my helpers.

One morning, I was about six months pregnant with David and really needed help with Jennifer. Because I was getting loud and disturbing his sleep, as he had just gone to bed, he jumped out of bed and grabbed two fists of hair and flung me towards the dresser, hitting my belly on the corner. Later in the day, two clumps of hair came out of my head and I started to spot. That was the beginning of the physical abuse.

I left Tom in 1988 after he choked me, threatened to kill me and raped me in our bedroom where David, 2, was sleeping. The children and I moved in with his sister. Tom called constantly and begged me to return. He promised that he had changed.

I wanted to believe him. Our children were 2 and 4; I wasn't sure how I would survive on my own. Tom begged me to return and promised never to hurt me again. After about eight weeks, I relented.

Tom's promises lasted only a few months. By 1990, he had installed a surveillance camera in the house so he could watch me on a TV screen from his office downstairs. He forced me to sleep with the camera pointed at me because he was convinced I was letting men come through my bedroom window. When he left the house, he put a locking device on my car's steering wheel so I couldn't leave. If I arrived home late from work, he forced me to undress so he could inspect my body for signs of sex.

When Jennifer and David were 6 and 4, I found the courage to call the police because Tom had spit in my face and threatened to kill me. When police arrived, they asked Tom if he threatened to kill me, and he said he had. Tom told them that I was his wife and he would say whatever he wished to me. The police then asked me to leave. I didn't understand why I had to be the one to leave, but quietly said okay and went to gather the children. The police told me that I had to leave for safety reasons but I couldn't take the children out of their home. I left our home without my kids, and I went home the next day and apologized to my husband because I needed to be with my children.

I was trapped. Tom's behavior was simply a continuation of what he had seen as a child. He told me that he had grown up in an abusive home and that he had once sat on the steps with a shotgun trying to find the courage to shoot his father as he yelled and hit Tom's mother. His lack of courage simply reaffirmed what his father had told him all his life: that he was worthless.

Still, I didn't tell my family what Tom was doing. It was too humiliating. By then, Tom was self-employed and making a six-digit salary. We lived in a nice home in a safe neighborhood, with the school within walking distance. My salary was in the 20s. How could I possibly make ends meet without Tom? I rationalized that as long as he was hurting only me, I could endure until the kids were a little older and out of daycare.

My family knew Tom was strange. On several occasions my parents took the children and me to Disney World, but Tom wouldn't go. My father described Tom as a loner who had no friends.

"If we would go down on a Sunday (to Lynn and Tom's house), we'd have dinner. He would come up (from the basement), fix his plate and take it down below to his office," my Dad recalled.

He balked if I asked him to watch the children for an hour while I went to the grocery store or ran some other errand. Spending time with his children would separate him from his television, computer or making model boats, so he instructed me not to "dump" the children on him.

I might have thought I kept my abuse from my parents, but my father knew.

"One time I knew he hit her," Ed Monk said. "He started spouting off. I said, 'Keep your big mouth shut or I'll come down there and shut it for you.'"

Life for the children and me was like walking on eggshells. We never knew what would set Tom off. He often slept all day and roamed the house at night. The children couldn't invite friends in. My friends stopped coming around because they couldn't stand Tom. Neighbors were polite, but kept their distance. My friends who knew of the abuse were supportive, but beginning to tire of my lack of movement toward permanently ending the relationship.

I was so beaten down over the years that I began to believe that I wasn't a good person, mom or wife. I tried to simply stay under the radar and keep my mouth shut. Eventually, I turned to alcohol as a way to cope. Tom couldn't stand to be around drunks. I spent many Friday and Saturday nights drunk or passed out. The alcohol numbed me. The alcohol gave me the courage to tell him how much I hated him and that he was a worthless husband, father and poor excuse for a human being.

Each time he would go out, I prayed that I would receive a call that he was in a fatal car crash. I wanted him to die so I could have an out.

As time went on, I knew that I would have to find the strength to end this pitiful marriage. Eventually I stopped arguing, asking, nagging and analyzing, as I no longer cared. He would say nasty things, would threaten to not make car payments, not do certain things and I would simply say, "Do whatever you want. I don't care."

We had about a year of calm before the storm. My lack of caring bothered him because he knew he was losing control over me. I acted like he no longer existed. The kids and I simply stayed out of his way. When he would be in one of his rare good moods, I still ignored him.

Around 1991, I began having an affair with a married man who also was struggling. The affair lasted about two years. It certainly was not one of my proudest moments, but it was definitely a turning point for me. Of course, I was being used and was devastated that in the end he didn't leave his wife for me. At the time, I thought this man was fun, engaging, complimentary and thoughtful and he made me feel good about myself. After years with Tom, it didn't take much to win me over. Still, I believe this relationship helped to rebuild my self-esteem, made my life more bearable and gave me hope that I deserved better.

After months of being ignored, Tom decided he wanted me out of the house. The man who had never been a husband or father decided he would raise his children without their mother. He tried baiting me, but I wouldn't fight back, other than to tell him he was sick and needed help.

In June of 1992, after I told Tom he was crazy if he thought I would ever leave our children to be raised by him, he followed me into the bedroom. When I went for the phone, he ripped it out of the wall, climbed on top of me, punched me multiple times in the chest and used the telephone cord to choke me. As I started to black out, he released his grip. Finally, I had endured enough. This time I didn't call the police. Instead, I brought the children into my bedroom and shoved a bureau in front of the door. The next morning, while Tom was sleeping, I packed the children's clothes and took them to my parents' house.

In my mind, it was finally over. The moment I made that decision, I couldn't believe how the weight lifted off me. It felt like several cinder blocks had been removed from my shoulders.

The next day I filed for a Protection from Abuse Order. Although it was granted, the judge, unbelievably, said both Tom and I could stay in the house until a hearing could be held in two weeks. I opted for safety and went to my parents' house.

In court, I was asked intimate details about my marriage. I felt like a tourist attraction. My family and friends didn't know even half of what I had been through and now I needed to say it in front of a courtroom full of strangers.

As I began to tell my story, Tom stopped the proceedings and agreed to accept the conditions of the PFA and move out of our home.

The months that followed were extremely difficult, with custody, child support and property proceedings. Child support payments came infrequently, and the debt Tom owed grew larger. Tom reasoned that since I wanted the divorce, everything was my fault. I had ruined his life, so why should he support our children?

Still, the children and I flourished. I was promoted to a management position with an increase in salary. David started kindergarten, and Jen loved the idea that it was okay to have friends come over to her house to play and even sleep over. We felt free.

On June 30, 1993, I received my divorce decree in the mail. A few friends came over to my house to celebrate, and I told them, "Men! Never again. Who needs them?" Four days later, at a neighbor's July 4 picnic, I met Paul. Although I am somewhat shy and timid, I found myself talking to Paul nonstop for 10 hours. Over the next 18 months, our relationship developed. Paul filled a void for Jen, Dave and me that we never knew had existed. We did more together as a family in those months than Jen and Dave had experienced in their lives. We went to amusement parks, waterparks, David's ball games, Harrisburg Senators minor league baseball games and on "haunted" hayrides. We played Wiffle Ball and captured lightning bugs in the backyard. I thought, "This is how life is supposed to be, enjoying moments and creating memories with those you love."

During most of this time, Jen and Dave's relationship with their father was almost nonexistent. I can remember the kids calling him, but he would rarely answer the phone. Then, about September 1994, Tom expressed an interest in seeing the kids and started to build a relationship with them. From September to December, he treated Jen and Dave better than he ever had. He began taking them on Sundays for the day. He would take them to dinner, help them study, take them to church, rent movies that they would watch together. He acted like a dad. I was happy for the kids.

Christmas 1994 was approaching, and Paul, the children and I were busy gearing up for the big day. During the week leading up to Christmas, we went to a hockey game and a Christmas program at school in which Jennifer played the clarinet. Jen finished wrapping presents for me. To satisfy David, who loved playing Monopoly, we set up the board in a corner of the living room and played for one hour every night. On Thursday Jen and I continued our traditional Christmas cookie baking. David would walk by casually to snatch a few.

On Friday night, we decided to go to the movies. We flipped a coin to decide between "Richie Rich" or "Dumb and Dumber." "Richie Rich" won. To save on movie treats, Jen and I popped three bags of popcorn and stuffed them into two large empty pocketbooks along with other junk food and soda and off we went.

That night we stayed up until midnight playing and talking. David headed off to bed, then returned to say, "I love you, Mom."

Saturday, Jen and I finished making cakes and pies for the family gathering on Christmas Day. Tom arrived early to pick up the children for the night. Although I had fought for no visitation with Tom, the judge would not agree to that or to supervised visitation. To this day, the words of that judge play over and over in my mind: "Mother, just because he may have hurt you doesn't mean he will hurt the children." The custody agreement allowed Tom to see them three Sundays a month and one night a year, alternating between Christmas Eve and Christmas night.

Tom arrived in a pleasant mood. He joked with the children and told them to get dressed up because he was taking them out to dinner. David had trouble finding pants to wear. All those Christmas cookies he had eaten made it difficult for him to zip his pants. David and I laughed. I made faces while I tried to zip his pants. We laughed harder. Finally, I had David lay on the bed while I zipped the pants. But we just couldn't fasten the button, so he left the pants unbuttoned and pulled on a sweater. Then Tom and the children walked out the door.

Jennifer, however, came back into the house twice to get things she had forgotten. On her third return, I raised my voice a bit and said, "Jen, now that's enough! What did you forget this time?" Jen said, "I forget to kiss you and tell you how much I love you!"

Those would be her last words to me.

Chapter 3

Nancy Recalls Her Unwelcome Homecoming

Saturday, January 11, began as a special day in the home of my sister Linda, and her husband, Michael Wilson. They went to their Catholic church with their son, Michael, as he made his first penance. When they arrived home about 11 a.m., Mike checked the answering machine. A woman who lived across the street from me had called to tell them something was wrong at my daughter Randi's house. On her way home from the grocery store, my neighbor had seen police activity and yellow crime scene tape around the yard.

Mike decided to jump in his car and drive to Randi's. Linda wanted to go, but Mike dissuaded her. At 44, Linda was two-and-a-half months pregnant with their second child. Mike was determined to shield Linda from whatever tragedy he was about to face.

Randi's street was awash in police vehicles, forensic vans and an ambulance. Mike parked, walked up to the tape and yelled to a trio of men standing on the lawn. He told them he was Randi's uncle and her lawyer. As one of the detectives approached, Mike asked what was happening. Were Randi and Brian OK?

"Brian's OK," the detective said, "but Randi's not. She's dead."

"What do you mean she's dead?" Mike replied. "She's only 28 years old."

Then his knees buckled, and he squatted in the street. After a few moments, the detective walked him to a police car to talk. Randi was not only dead; she had been murdered.

"I couldn't focus," Mike said. Scenarios swirled through his brain, but "never once did I think it was Brian. Not at that moment."

Mike knew he would have to deliver the bad news to Linda and the rest of the family. But he wasn't ready. He needed time to collect his thoughts and try to pull himself together. He stopped at his parents' house on the way home, sat on their sofa, talked with his father and cried.

On the drive home, thoughts swirled. He wondered how he would tell Linda. She and Randi, just 15 years apart, had been like sisters. Would the news harm their unborn child?

How, he thought, would the news reach me? Mike knew I was on a cruise, but felt strongly that no one but family should bring me this awful news.

And what of my mother, Randi's grandmother? Randi had been her first grandchild. How would they tell her Randi was gone?

Despite their own pain, Mike and Linda jumped into action. They knew I was on the sixth day of a seven-day cruise to the Caribbean with my friend, Linda Morrison. They decided they had to track me down, find out exactly when I would arrive home and intercept me before I heard the news. Working two phone lines, they found the name of our cruise ship, made contact with the captain and arranged to tell Linda Morrison the news. They learned when the plane would land in Baltimore and arranged with the airline to have me whisked off the plane and directly into the arms of family.

Linda Morrison and I had spent Saturday on the cruise line's private island. When we returned to our cabin, we found a note asking Linda to go to the captain's office. Immediately we anticipated the worst. During a call home prior to departure, Linda had learned that her brother had been hospitalized with heart problems. This summons to the captain's office probably meant bad news.

I walked to the office with Linda, but the crew wouldn't allow me to accompany her inside. I was left worrying and wondering outside the door for 30 minutes.

Linda had walked into what looked to her like an interrogation room. Sterile, like the rooms you see on cop shows on TV, it held only a table, a phone, a pad and a pencil.

When they told her Michael Wilson wanted to speak with her, Linda was totally confused. She feared something had happened to my pregnant sister Linda.

At first, Mike wouldn't share his news. He made her promise she would not tell me what he was about to say.

Then he said, "Randi is dead."

Linda Morrison cried. She couldn't catch her breath. "This can't be real," she said. "What am I going to do?" Mike told her to keep me safe, keep me from the news.

"I wanted to go through the phone and choke him," Linda said. "I'm not equipped to do this. I'm an emotional person."

She looked at the others in the room and said, "I can't walk out that door. My friend is going to be out there, and I don't know what to tell her."

So she told me nothing. She walked out of the room crying, and I assumed it was her brother. Linda said little for the rest of the trip. She didn't look at me for the rest of that day and the next. All she told me was that we were to pack our belongings. When the ship pulled into port in Miami, we were to be the first passengers off. As a result, we could catch an earlier flight home.

I tried calling Randi from the airport. When no one answered, I tried calling my boyfriend, Greg Green. He didn't answer.

My relationship with Greg was fairly new at the time. We had met at work, where Greg was a human resources director. I had introduced him to Randi and Brian at a cookout. After that meeting, the four of us attended high school football games and spent time together as couples. We shared Christmas Eve dinner just two weeks before Randi was murdered.

My brother-in-law Mike called Greg to tell him about Randi's murder. He was devastated by the news. "I got off the phone and I cried. I just could not believe that God would let this happen. I knew how much this would hurt her. Randi was her life," he said.

Greg decided to drive to the Baltimore airport to be part of the support system waiting for me.

Meanwhile, Linda Morrison and I boarded the plane for the flight home. She put on her headphones and buried herself in music. Although I looked forward to arriving home, my thoughts were tempered by worries about my friend. Her silence had really frustrated me, and I felt guilty because I couldn't find any words to comfort her.

Several miserable hours later, when I stood up to leave the plane; I heard my name called over the loudspeaker. I was told to go to the information desk. Then a woman with a walkie-talkie verified my name and ushered me toward what the airport calls a meditation room, where she said my sister Patty would be waiting. My heart raced. I couldn't understand why Patty would be at the airport. My first thought was that something had happened to our sister Linda. Silently, I prayed that everything would be all right. When the door opened, my eyes scanned the room. I saw Patty, my mother, my brother-in-law. Then it hit me. Where was Randi?

Suddenly, everyone moved toward me as if to form a protective shield. As my mother and sister ran to me, I heard the words, "Something has happened to Randi." Randi was gone. Randi was dead. How? Why? Then someone said her husband, Brian, was OK. I turned my head slightly and saw my sister Linda, standing, watching, and suddenly I knew it was true.

I threw a fit like a child. I stomped my feet, took off my jacket and flung it across the room. I walked over to a wall and pounded my fists repeatedly. It couldn't be. Not Randi. Not my only child. Not my best friend, the daughter who was my world.

Greg was there, as was Linda Morrison. Basking in horror, I didn't see them. I was blinded by anger and loss.

All I remember is a long ride home. My family had brought pictures of Randi, which I held in my lap. I remember talking and crying on the phone with Brian, the son-in-law I loved like a son. Brian had found Randi when he returned from dinner with a friend on Friday. Randi had been stabbed repeatedly and was dead on the garage floor.

I begged to see Randi. All I wanted was to be with her, hold her hand, tell her that I was there and that I love her. But police wouldn't allow it. So I did the next best thing. I insisted we drive past Randi's house. But I couldn't go in there either. The house that Randi loved was surrounded by yellow crime tape. I couldn't see the daughter I loved or find comfort inside her home. I remember sitting in the car and crying. I wanted Randi to come to the front door, just as bubbly as ever, happy that we all came to see her. I remember silence in the car; no one said anything.

As we sat there, I noticed the lights were lit on Randi's Christmas tree. I wondered who had done that because Randi never left her lights on.

Randi. Beautiful Randi. Who would want to hurt Randi?

My mother stayed with me that first night home. She tried to comfort me as we talked into the night. When we finally went to bed, my brain filled with jumbled thoughts. I must have drifted off to sleep for a short time, because I dreamed I had seen Randi. She was standing above my bed and looked like an angel. Then she spread her beautiful white wings and said, "Mom, I'm okay, and I will take care of you."

Randi, my angel, promised to care for me as I had always cared for her. She had been just five when I left her father, and from then on, it had been just the two of us. I always kept her close; she was shielded and protected.

When she graduated from Catholic high school, Randi went to college in Bloomsburg, Pa., where she studied to be a speech pathologist. In 1995, while applying to work at a day care on her summer break, she met Brian Trimble. Two years later, they became engaged. Their plan was to marry in 2000, after Randi had her master's degree and a job in her field.

Not long after, Randi noticed that Brian seemed to be slurring his words. With Randi's encouragement, Brian's mother took him to a doctor. They returned with bad news: Brian had multiple sclerosis.

With the diagnosis, we believed that Brian was fragile, so we treated him like that.

I talked seriously with my daughter about the future with Brian. Maybe they shouldn't marry. Randi was opening herself to life as nursemaid to her husband. But Randi wouldn't consider breaking their engagement. She was convinced that Brian wouldn't leave her if the tables were turned.

Randi, a planner, like me, anticipated a future in which Brian's disability would overtake him. A year before the wedding, Randi bought a house a few blocks from me. She worked both full-time and part-time as a speech pathologist. She held a third job on Sunday mornings at a nearby flea market. She saved money for the rainy days the couple expected to come eventually.

Despite prodding from Randi and me, Brian had never finished college. He switched jobs several times, eventually landing on the IT help desk at Capital Blue Cross.

During the three years they were engaged, Randi carefully planned her wedding. She and Brian opened a bank account to save money for the wedding and honeymoon. She arranged to hold the wedding ceremony at Saint Joseph's Church in Mechanicsburg and the reception at the Carlisle Country Club. She secured permission to have photographs taken at the Ryan Building at the Pennsylvania Capitol, regarded as one of the most beautiful in the country.

Within a few weeks of her engagement, Randi picked out a wedding gown with a sweetheart neckline, fitted waist and a large bow on the back. She wore that dress, and her megawatt smile, as she walked down the aisle on the arm of my Uncle Primo.

My nephew Michael, about six years old at the time, said she looked like Cinderella.

Randi's marriage could not break the bond between mother and daughter. That bond is outlined in a 19-page letter I wrote just before Randi's college graduation in May 1997. "You are my soul mate. We share things that only you and I will understand. After so many years of being together you begin to think alike and know what the other is thinking. We really do have a lot in common – we like the same music (well except for a few country songs), we like to laugh, we like to have our private time, we are hard workers, we have a lot of perseverance, we are well organized, and we are very sentimental. Not bad.

"Don't try to hide your feelings with me because I will sense what is wrong. I guess that is because I have always promised to be there when you needed me. Ironically, I needed to know you were there, and I was in your thoughts. I believe we will be soul mates forever."

Randi's happiness increased after her marriage. She was so much in love with Brian. She had a great job, loved her home and was trying so hard to have a child.

All of that ended on a January night. Someone was waiting for Randi. When she stepped out of her car in her garage, a man tried to strangle her with an electrical cord from a Christmas tree ornament. She fought back, but the intruder pulled a knife, stabbed her 27 times and cut her throat. Brian found Randi dead on the garage floor.

The police questioned Brian intensely, as they do when a spouse is murdered. But he had an alibi. He was in Lancaster, at least 40 miles away, eating dinner with a friend. Still, he felt responsible, he told me through his tears. Fridays were usually their date night. But that morning he had argued with Randi. Then, someone from Randi's part-time job, which she worked Tuesdays and Thursdays, had called and asked her to work that evening. The couple had talked in the afternoon, and

Brian went out with a friend. Brian told me he felt it was his fault because he hadn't been there for Randi.

Guilt gripped me, too. Why had I gone on a cruise? Could I have prevented this horror if I had stayed home?

I felt lost, sad. When I looked at Randi's photos, our eyes locked. My daughter seemed to be telling me something. What could it be?

The following day, Brian and his family came to my house. I wanted to talk to him privately so I could learn every detail of my daughter's final minutes. I asked if it was possible that Randi was still alive when he returned home. Since Randi and Brian both knew CPR, I wondered if he had tried to save her.

People had suggested to me that a husband, finding his wife bleeding on the floor, would touch her, stroke her, listen for a pulse or a sign of breathing. Brian said he did none of those things. He told me he never touched Randi, that he just knew she was dead.

None of that made me suspicious. Neither did his response that he had arrived home at 8:10. He might have said, "Just after 8," or "Between 8 and 8:15." Instead he was very precise. I wasn't thinking that he might need an alibi.

After the police arrived, Brian had called his mother to tell her Randi had been murdered. He called no one in our family because, he said, he didn't want to upset them.

Despite my own aching pain, I worried about Brian. He was, after all, fragile.

On the Monday after Randi was murdered, Brian, my brother-in-law Mike and I went to the police station for what would become a two-and-a-half-hour interrogation. Police wanted to know everything about Randi. They called it "building a victimology." I remember little more than fear. What I learned from the police brought new horror.

I wrote that night in my journal, "How could someone stab my baby over and over? That never left my mind the rest of the night. I cried outside and I cried internally, thinking that my baby girl was hurt so bad, lying on cold cement bleeding to death. Was she alive, fighting for her life?"

That night, my eyes fell on Randi's wedding gown. I decided my daughter should be buried in the dress she had worn on the happiest day of her life.

The next day Brian met again with detectives and a forensic specialist, so I was without him as I planned my only child's funeral. Three-and-a-half-hours passed as I selected a casket, arranged times, picked out cards, prayers, flowers and music for an event I dreaded. When all was done, I wrote the obituary. Should it say Randi Trimble, 28, of Camp Hill died? Or should it say she was murdered? Did it matter?

I stayed up all night to write that obituary. I've read a million obituaries in my life and I couldn't even think what to write for my daughter.

Eventually, I decided on the word "murder." The obituary also noted that Randi was survived by her "devoted husband" and "loving mother." Those who wished to make memorial contributions could send them to National Multiple Sclerosis, an organization that Brian might need someday.

Randi was gone, and I knew with certainty that my life would never be the same.

I had arranged for a private viewing for friends and family prior to the visitation at the funeral home. It would be the last time I would see Randi. A message came from the funeral home, delivered by my sister, Patty: When it was time for the viewing, we weren't to touch Randi, other than her hands.

What mother wants to know that her daughter's body is in such delicate condition? During my private time with Randi, I saw the damage.

That night I wrote in my journal, "I looked at my baby – her face so swollen. They told me earlier that they had to reconstruct her forehead – not to touch her. That was not Randi, so swollen. It was as if they painted her face, her forehead so high, and her hair wasn't the way she would have liked it. I saw bruises on her left arm, so prominent. I could tell that they tried to cover them up, but the bruises were so bad. Oh, my God, the cuts on her hands were not covered. Her lips so swollen. How awful."

Brian and I had planned to cover Randi's body with a blanket when the private viewing concluded at 5 p.m. But Brian had left with his family to go to a nearby Friendly's restaurant, and it fell to me to cover my child for the last time. Through my tears I realized the symbolism of the pink blanket. Just as I had covered my daughter with a pink blanket the first day home after her birth, I would cover her for the last time. Alone. Just Randi and I, as it had been for so many years.

That evening, I stood and greeted each of the more than 300 people who attended Randi's visitation. I didn't know it then, but among the visitors, among the people I hugged, was the man who had murdered my daughter.

At the viewing, my mother, sisters and Greg kept their eyes on me. I remember looking up and seeing Greg standing in the lobby. He made me feel safe.

At one point I turned to Brian and reminded him that we had to be strong for Randi, and we had to find out who killed her.

Despite my own pain, I was determined to provide support for my son-in-law. My most important concern was Brian. I had no inkling then that Brian knew who had killed Randi or that my indescribable pain was destined to get worse.

Greg harbored suspicions about Brian almost from the start. He was a step removed from Randi, Brian and me. He wasn't family. Perhaps that's why he was quick to notice early on that things just didn't feel right.

Greg thought Brian was acting from the beginning and throughout the viewing, visitation and funeral.

"Theatrically, it was a performance beyond belief," he said.

It bothered him that Brian was unavailable to make funeral arrangements, and then, rather than help me pull the blanket over Randi, he left the visitation before it ended and went to Friendly's with his family.

On the evening of the visitation, he kept his eye on Brian. "He was hanging out with this guy, and it was nothing you would expect of a man who just lost his wife. The sorrow, the grief, it just wasn't there. And then he left," he said.

Our co-worker, Samantha Krepps, felt that Brian was playing a role. "I remember seeing him hugging people, and he saw me out of the corner of his eye. He looked at Randi's picture on the casket and mouthed, 'I love you.'"

It seemed rehearsed, she said.

Greg and Mike Wilson noticed that Brian's co-worker stayed through the entire visitation. He sat alone the whole time.

Samantha noticed him, too. And she recalled thinking, "Who is that weirdo?"

They would learn later he was Blaine Norris, Brian's co-worker, who had hugged me just days after he had murdered my daughter. I also learned later that detectives had been present at the visitation watching Brian.

Brian played on how weak he felt as the two of us stood for hours during the visitation. I recall both his mother and his father saying, at different times, how difficult this was for Brian. He was feeling so weak he had to lie down in the back room. Several people observed how Brian went into a small back room and called in friends to comfort him. One of them was Blaine Norris.

Months later I learned that as Brian was walking back to "rest," he stopped to talk to a young woman. Someone overheard him say, "When all of this is over, we need to go dancing."

The next day at the funeral, Greg said Brian and his friends acted as if they were at a party. His suspicions heightened.

Linda Morrison noticed, too. "He didn't seem like he was grieving," Linda said. "I just thought he's just frigging weird."

After the funeral, when everyone gathered at my house, Brian came in and walked to the head of the food line. He was overheard saying, "I guess I can break in because I'm the guest of honor."

Brian continued to fuel the flames in the days and weeks ahead. It was the little things people noticed.

My sister, Rose, found herself alone with Brian at my kitchen table, when he mentioned he had been spending a lot of time playing video games. "Don't tell Mamacita," he said, "but I bought an Xbox."

During the week after Randi's murder, both Brian and I were constantly surrounded by family members with questions. What should they do about this? How should they handle that? I slept little and ate less. I lost weight.

Brian went to stay with his mother. He took Randi's pet dog, Monique, with him, saying she would help him preserve Randi's memory.

Then the day after we buried Randi, his mother enlisted my help in talking Brian out of moving to an apartment. I couldn't understand his haste to move into an apartment. He said he no longer wanted to live in the house full of memories he had shared with Randi. His mother and I agreed he was being hasty.

I told Brian he could move in with me. I said I would take care of him. But he was insistent and moved into an apartment within a few weeks.

"Based on his actions and everything I observed, I started getting this sick feeling," Greg said. "I thought if he's responsible, it will be the ultimate betrayal."

I noticed small things as well, but I dismissed them or made excuses for Brian.

On January 27, I noted that Brian stopped by the house wearing his stepsister's jacket. "Strange," I wrote.

Months later, I learned Brian was having an affair with his stepsister.

Also "strange" was an incident on February 1. Brian said he would be spending the weekend at his father's house in Maryland. When I called there for him, his father said he wasn't there. The next day Brian said, "I was in the other room. Of course I was there."

I felt that Brian was being less than honest. He didn't want me asking where he was. When I learned he was taking extra bereavement time, he insisted it was because his boss had recommended it. Around the same time, Rose told me she had called Brian Saturday, the day after Randi's murder, and he was at the movies with his father and brother.

Brian bought a new car, went out with friends and changed his appearance. When talking to me, he referred to Randi as "your daughter," not as "my wife." Pretty soon, he stopped calling me altogether.

But as we proceeded to settle Randi's estate, I wrote in my journal, "I want to make sure that Brian is secure for the remainder of his natural life with money in case his MS is flaring up."

My brother-in-law Mike had advised Brian and me that I should be executor of the estate to alleviate any problems until he was cleared by police. Police told me they would turn over Randi's house on January 28. I had to prepare myself to walk into the house without Randi. I knew the effect it would have on my emotions. I simply couldn't imagine walking into that empty house alone. So I called Brian and arranged for us to go in together. I asked him not to go into the house without me, and not to bring his parents. I hoped that the two of us, mother and husband, walking in together would feel Randi's presence in the home she had loved.

I raced to the house from work around 4:15 to meet the police officer, and saw Randi's Ford Escape parked in the driveway. As I walked toward the house I could hear Brian's mother inside, talking to the police. When I went inside, I sat on the couch and cried. I missed Randi so much. Maybe, I thought, if I sat very still, my daughter would walk around the corner from the kitchen as she had a hundred times before.

Brian and I walked to the bedrooms, where clothes were thrown all over the floor, the dresser drawers were turned upside down and the contents of the file cabinet lay on the floor. Untouched and hanging on the bedpost was Randi's rosary. What had the murderer wanted? I wondered.

As mother and husband, we walked through the house. Soon we approached the door to the garage. Brian stopped and stared as I looked on in fear, terrified that I might still see my daughter's body there. Instead, I saw splatters of blood on the door. On the dining room table were Randi's empty purse, her mittens and sunglasses.

Before we left, Brian wanted to pick up a few things. I assumed he would get clothes for work. Instead he took computer equipment. Then we sat on the floor in front of the TV as he went through a cabinet filled with CDs and DVDs, picking what he wanted.

"Mamacita," he said, "I promised you that I would take care of Randi and look what happened." He cried. I cried and promised him that we would find out who killed Randi.

The days and weeks that followed continued to be times of despair. My pain is evident in the entries I wrote in the journal I had begun when Randi was born: "I could not eat, did not want to eat. I don't want to go on like this. I am so lonely. Oh, Randi, please come home to me. Tell me that this was all a mistake; that this did not happen. I can't stand that someone hurt you."

On January 16, at 11:43 p.m., someone called my house and said, "Hello," loudly. Then there was silence. I panicked. "Please, God," I wrote in my journal, "don't let that be the killer. I am so frightened."

Now, I believed the killer was stalking me. I was terrified to be alone, so my mother slept in my house. I asked friends to follow me home, to accompany me to the grocery store. I checked every room in my house, peeked into the shower stall, kept my blinds and curtains closed. I was terrified of the garage.

My first day back at work, I received a disturbing email, sent from a webmail server that Brian had set up several years earlier. It said, "This is an excite game, this game is my first work, you are my first player, I wish you would enjoy it."

I was shaken, horrified. That webmail server had been set up to deliver messages from Randi. Now, it seemed, her killer was taunting me.

When I reported it, Capitol police seized my computer. I was told to park in a different space every day. I was ordered to have someone escort me to my car. My fear heightened. Even with the drapes drawn and doors locked, I no longer felt safe in my home.

When state police investigated the source of the email sent to me, they traced it to a laptop in a dorm at Indiana University of Pennsylvania. Students there told them the laptop had been stolen. Police could never connect Brian to the laptop or the students, but I continue to believe he was involved somehow.

Linda Morrison stayed with me much of the time.

"She was afraid to be in public. She was afraid to go anywhere," Linda recalled.

My fear of the unknown was horrible, but I was about to discover that reality can be even worse.

Chapter 4

The Aftermath

Brian's involvement in Randi's death may have blind-sided me, but police suspected him from the moment they responded to his 911 call. Brian had found Randi dead in their garage between 8 and 8:30 p.m. on January 10, 2003.

Their house on Wood Street had been ransacked. Items were thrown around the three bedrooms and removed from clos-ets, an entertainment system in the living room and a hutch in the dining room. Everything was disturbed except Brian's prized computer station. Brian told police that an open push-out window in the kitchen might have provided access for a burglar.

Detectives didn't believe it. The window opening was too small, only about 10 inches, and no one could have entered without disturbing items on a table beneath it. Also, detectives thought, why would a burglar come through the window and push it partially shut, cutting off an escape route? And the ran-sacking wasn't right. Burglars don't just ransack; they search. Why would a burglar scatter the cleaning products under the bathroom sink? And why would a burglar kill Randi rather than flee? She had entered the house through the garage. The opening garage door made enough noise to be heard anywhere in the house, leaving a burglar time to get away.

Although detectives suspected Brian, he had an alibi. He had been eating dinner with a friend 40 miles away at the Park City Mall in Lancaster when Randi died. Still, they believed he had a hand in Randi's murder.

At 9 p.m. on February 7 – about a month after Randi's murder -- I received a phone call that changed everything I believed. The lead detectives wanted to see me immediately in the district attorney's office. Now was the time when they needed my cooperation, they said. They told me where to park and what entrance to use. I learned later that Brian was being questioned at the same time, and they didn't want him to see me.

My brother-in-law, Mike, who normally would have accompanied me, was out of town on duty with the National Guard that weekend. But Linda Morrison had followed me home after the two of us ate dinner and was still at my house. With my anxiety soaring, Linda offered to go with me.

What we learned that night once again put Linda in the uncomfortable position she had found herself in on the cruise ship. She would know things she could not discuss.

The detectives swore Linda and me to secrecy. They said Brian and two others were downstairs being questioned. "Why Brian?" I wondered. But my questions turned to tears as the detectives told me what they believed to be true.

Brian was their primary suspect. He may not have killed Randi, but he was definitely involved, as far as detectives were concerned. They said it was common knowledge among Brian's friends that he wanted a divorce. He had told people at work that he and Randi couldn't stand to be in the same room. He said she could have the house, but he wanted his video games, videos, computer and half the money in their joint account.

It was as if Randi had been murdered again. I was devastated. I wrote in my journal, "I hate him. No wonder nothing was being done to clear him. Why would Brian kill Randi –

money? I had never once thought that Brian would do this. He loved Randi, adored her."

I knew that if Randi had known Brian wanted a divorce, she would have told me. Randi wouldn't have tried for months to get pregnant if she knew.

Linda and I were told we must keep this information to ourselves while police built their case. I could confide in Mike. But not being able to tell the rest of my family or friends was devastating. I felt that I was betraying my family, just as Brian had, by not telling them.

But Greg knew just by looking at me.

He said the look on my face was a mirror image of how I had reacted to news of Randi's death. I vowed at that moment never again to refer to Brian as my son-in-law. I wanted him to rot in hell.

My hell would continue through March and April and into May. I was forced to play a role and live a lie. Police wanted me to act normal. I was supposed to pretend things were fine between Brian and me. I had to take his phone calls and listen to him say, "Please don't think that I hurt her. I love her so much." I had to grimace if he called me Mamacita. I had to remember my daughter's wedding, the last Christmas we had spent together, and know that the third person in the pictures, the man my daughter loved, was a killer. I had to live with the knowledge that I did everything for Brian and he betrayed me.

I kept the secret. But one day I went to the mall with Samantha to replace a cell phone I had lost. We stopped at Subway to eat. I looked at Samantha and said, "They have a suspect and I can't say."

Samantha said, "It's him." I didn't say a word, but she knew.

Just when I thought Brian couldn't hurt me anymore, he called one day and said he was going to give me Randi's treasured dog, Monique. I said fine, but told him that I wouldn't be home until later.

Brian came over anyway and tried to drop the dog off with my neighbor, Kim. But Kim wasn't home. Her mother, who was babysitting, refused to take Monique. So Brian, who was with his stepsister, drove to the house on Wood Street. The locks had been changed and I had the keys. In an effort to get in, he broke the new lock and kicked in the side door to the garage. I could not believe that he would want to walk into the garage where Randi once lay.

He eventually left Monique with a neighbor near the Wood Street house.

When I finally retrieved Monique, she was filthy and shaking, which only infuriated me more.

Later, when I asked why he had damaged the house in an effort to get in, he said he had wanted to pick up a couple of his things. I suspect he wanted to see what police had confiscated.

By then he already knew that police had taken his computer and sent it to their crime lab. I can't imagine what else was so important.

When state police, using warrants, took Brian's computer, they found some interesting things. He had downloaded an online publication called "Hit Man On Line," a 54-page, article written by "Rex Feral." The technical manual describes several methods of committing murder.

Police noted that eight days before Randi was murdered, Brian had sent the manual to Blaine Norris. Among the book's suggestions is staging a robbery at a murder scene to throw police off the killer's trail.

I spent several tension-filled months waiting to see when Brian would be arrested. By then, I knew he had masterminded the plot to kill Randi. Police kept me informed. They called me late one evening and told me they wanted to exhume Randi's body. I wasn't quite sure what that meant, but I didn't think they could do it without my permission. They also planned to tell Brian they might exhume Randi's body, hoping it would get him to confess.

After all the emotional distress, police later told me that the exhumation threat had been a ploy.

Finally, police told me that they intended to ask Brian, his parents and his brother to go to the district attorney's office. They thought if they questioned him in front of his family, he might confess.

Instead, he went in with just his mother on May 8 and answered their questions. Then, he asked his mother to leave the room, and he confessed. Saving his own hide was foremost in his mind. He agreed to describe the events leading up to Randi's murder if prosecutors would take the death penalty off the table.

The following morning I jumped out of bed and turned on the news, hoping to hear news of Brian's arrest. I scanned the channels and heard nothing. I remember feeling completely drained.

I met Greg for breakfast and went to work. My sisters called to check on me. Then Samantha called and said District Attorney Skip Ebert had held a news conference at 10 a.m. to announce that Brian Trimble had been arrested at 2:20 a.m. and had been denied bail. He was charged with criminal homicide, first degree murder, criminal solicitation to commit homicide, criminal conspiracy to commit murder, criminal attempt to commit insurance fraud and insurance fraud.

I cried.

Brian had told police he was frustrated with his wife and had shared his feelings with Blaine Norris, another computer technician at Capital Blue Cross. Blaine, who was shooting a horror movie on the Appalachian Trail, had wanted Brian to invest money in the film and participate as videographer. Randi had said no to both requests. Then he had asked to borrow Brian's expensive photography equipment for the movie. Again, Randi said no.

Talk of killing Randi began as early as May 2002. Brian frequently complained that Randi wouldn't allow him to do things with friends. "Well, you could kill her," Blaine suggested. They laughed it off and dropped the subject for a time.

Brian's complaints continued. He considered divorce, but abandoned the idea. One day, as he was complaining at the water fountain at work, the idea was resurrected. Brian said it was his best course because a divorce would hurt Randi.

Their initial plan called for Blaine to kill Randi on Sunday, January 12, when she returned from work at the flea market around 1 p.m. Instead, the plot turned into action on January 10.

The night before, the two men had planned to join a group of friends and play Earth Dawn, a role-playing game similar to Dungeons and Dragons. Randi and Brian argued, and Brian didn't play the game.

Blaine was angry with his friend for not playing, and the next morning when he met Brian in the cafeteria at work, he said, "This is the day to do it."

Later that day, Brian let Blaine into his house, where the two staged a burglary. Blaine put pants, a shirt and a hooded black sweatshirt over his work clothes. He changed into black socks and sneakers and donned latex gloves topped with a pair of black gloves. He had a black mask, a knife strapped into a sheath on his leg and a .22 caliber gun in a holster on his other leg.

When Brian left for dinner with a friend to establish an alibi, Blaine waited. Eventually, Randi pulled into her garage and exited her car. Blaine wrapped an electric cord around her neck, but Randi fought back. Blaine, using a 6-inch serrated knife, stabbed her 27 times.

For his role, Blaine had been promised $20,000 from the proceeds of Randi's life insurance and reimbursement of any expenses incurred in the commission of the crime. The two men thought they might take a trip to Las Vegas where Blaine could increase his wealth by gambling. Either way, the money would ease him out of the debt he had incurred while trying to produce the horror movie.

Unbelievably, Brian told police he had Randi murdered because he didn't want to put his wife and her family through the pain of a divorce.

After I learned the truth about Brian, Greg compared what was happening to me to the Laci Peterson case playing on the news from California. Laci had disappeared on Christmas Eve, 2002. It wasn't until the following April that her body, and the body of her unborn son, washed onto shore. Her husband, Scott Peterson, eventually was found guilty of murdering Laci and their child and is on death row.

Like Peterson, Brian fooled a lot of people. He was, Greg said, like Jekyll and Hyde.

Since Brian made a deal to plead guilty and cooperate with police, there would be no trial for him.

Blaine Norris was arrested in October 2003, nine months after Randi's murder, and charged with the same crimes as Brian. He pleaded not guilty at his preliminary hearing, and his trial was set for June 7, 2004. However, like Brian, he agreed eventually to plead guilty if the death penalty was removed. The court took his guilty plea on April 19, 2004.

Both he and Brian were housed in the Cumberland County prison until their sentencings.

By the time Blaine Norris was sentenced, he had found religion and claimed the blood of Jesus had washed him free of sin.

"The weights of my sins, even murder, have been lifted. I'm free," Blaine said.

At his sentencing, he spoke for a long time about the emptiness of his life leading up to the murder of Randi. He described how he had found religion in prison and asked that my family and I try to find a way to forgive him.

In an attempt to explain what had happened, Blaine said, "I had so much darkness in me, so much hatred for myself, for the world, for everyone and everything. I just did not care about anything at all. I was utterly despicable, and I committed some of the worst sins and crimes known to the world.

"I was not always like that," the former Boy Scout said. "I was loving, happy, caring and gentle. I had goals and dreams. I had values and morals. I wanted what was right. So what went wrong? In a word, emptiness. For as long as I can remember, I felt like I was missing something. There was a hole inside me that I couldn't fill. Nothing could satisfy that undefinable need inside of me. I tried love, marriage, hobby after hobby, philosophy, my career, anything, but nothing worked. I was still empty. Nothing was wrong, but I was so unhappy."

Finding God, he said, changed that. ˙

But I was having none of it. I spoke at Blaine's sentencing, describing the beautiful and loving daughter who was my best friend and "the brutal murder caused by two monsters driven by greed."

I told the court that although I had lost my daughter, I would survive. It had been my mission for the last year and a half, to find the person who murdered my daughter, the killer, to make sure that he would not see another day of freedom.

Blaine may have killed Randi, but in my heart I blamed Brian for her murder. On October 6, 2004, I wrote these words in my journal: "Today I face the person that killed my daughter." For months, I had awaited this day, thinking, writing, preparing, practicing. I would go into a courtroom and tell Brian Trimble what he had done to me and all of those who loved Randi.

But first, I had to walk through a media frenzy. Reporters had gathered outside the courthouse to wait as Brian was sentenced to prison for life. The murder of my daughter, Randi, had been big news for months in Harrisburg and the surrounding area. The slaughter of a college-educated, attractive, hardworking young woman in the garage of her suburban home had prompted headlines and led the newscasts. The weird plot that led to her murder, the pact between two nerdy workers at one of the area's largest employers, was bizarre enough to be discussed on barstools and over dinner tables. Randi and I had unwillingly become the focus of news as a result of the evil actions of Randi's husband, Brian Trimble, and his co-worker, Blaine Norris.

It seemed so long ago, but once I had loved Brian. He called me Mamacita, a nickname that reflected my Mexican heritage. I welcomed him into my home and my heart because he was the man Randi loved and married. We shared holidays. We shared Randi's love. I put aside my own anguish after Randi's murder so I could provide support for Brian. Poor Brian, the young widower. Until I learned the horrible truth.

Now I would go into a courtroom and have my say. I would tell the monster what I had lost because of him. I would describe the indescribable pain. I would tell him about the hole in my heart, the one no one or nothing could heal. I would talk about Randi, the daughter I loved more than myself. Today, finally, I would look Brian Trimble in the eyes and call him a monster.

I waited in the Victim Services office of the Cumberland County Courthouse with my family and my victim advocate, Donna Vandemortel. As we waited, I looked out the window on a crisp fall afternoon and wondered why I couldn't be one of the busy people attending to their mundane chores on the street. Why was I in this horrible place preparing to face this horrible man? Why had the fates chosen me to suffer this crushing blow? How could I go on without my precious daughter, Randi?

My eyes returned to the room. I saw my mother, wringing her hands in a fruitless effort to calm her nerves. I saw the sadness in my sisters' eyes as each, in her own way, relived those terrible days after Randi's death. I turned inward, repeating my mantra: "Don't give up. Randi would want you to be strong. Don't let him see you weak; don't let him win."

Not so long ago, I would have considered myself a winner. I had survived a violent marriage, found the strength to start a new life for myself and Randi, put us both through college and emerged as my daughter's best friend. I did right by Randi, and now I had time for myself, time to travel and to be with friends. My daughter was married, happy, living nearby and talking about making me a grandmother. Meanwhile, I was enjoying my job and my friends and moving forward with a relationship that seemed very right.

That was then. Now gray clouded my world. Randi was gone and nothing would ever be right again. Although I no longer felt like a winner, I was still a strong, determined woman, and today I would have my say.

When it was time, my family and I walked into the courtroom where friends of Randi and other supporters had gathered. Although I sat, my body shook uncontrollably. My mother placed her hand gently on my knee in a futile effort to calm my shaking. "It will be OK," my mother whispered. "We are here for you; we love you."

As my mother worried about me, I worried about her. She was 72 years old. How difficult it must have been for her to walk into a courtroom for the first time in her life and face her granddaughter's killer.

Not that I was an expert. All I knew about courtrooms had come from watching *Perry Mason*. Thank goodness for Donna, my victim advocate, who never left my side.

Donna had mentored me, discussing how I should write my impact statement and explaining what would happen in the courtroom. Victims can provide an impact statement either written or orally. But I wanted to talk. I wanted to face Brian and tell him, the judge, the attorneys and the public how this crime affected me.

I felt prepared, knowing that I had read and reread my statement at least 20 times and rehearsed it a million times in my head. No matter what I said, the deal to send Brian away for life would not be revoked. But I just needed him to leave the courtroom hearing my voice and replaying my message over and over.

Then, from the corner of my eye I saw him. Brian, the murderer. Brian, the monster. Brian, shuffling in shackles, his head shaven, his eyes dark. He looked like the embodiment of evil, and I hated him.

In the courtroom, Brian had confessed to his plot to murder Randi. He had asked me to forgive him. He said he loved Randi, as well as his family and friends. He said he had found God. He turned to those assembled in the courtroom, including me and my family, and said, "I love you all." He never shed a tear.

That day, in that courtroom, Brian was sentenced to spend the rest of his life in a Pennsylvania prison, and I got the opportunity to spew out the words I had practiced. With determination, I read my statement: "I look at Brian Trimble face to face with a great amount of courage. I am finally facing the person who truly murdered my precious daughter Randi. His remorse will mean nothing to me. His sorrow is only regret and the reality of knowing that he got caught and that he will spend the remainder of his life in prison. But now it's my turn, and I've searched in my heart for what I wanted to say to Brian and to let him know all the pain and suffering I have endured. I want him to look around and see those people and all of her friends that support Randi and loved Randi. Look around the room and look at the eyes of her grandmother and her aunts, and her cousins and her best friends and see the sorrow that he has inflicted on them. This is the message I want him to live with the remainder of his life. He is calculating. He's diabolical. He's evil. He's a monster."

As I spoke, Brian turned toward me and nodded, as if to say, "Yes, Mamacita, you are right."

I watched as Brian was handcuffed. He looked at me in a cunning way, as if to show that an itsy bitsy part of him knew that he had destroyed any chance at happiness for the rest of his life. His look simply told me that he was doing what he was always good at – manipulating everyone to believe he was the victim.

Not this time.

I knew I would not feel sorry for him, but those thousand voices in my head were asking, "Was I truly rid of him? Should I forgive him?"

"Don't be so gullible," I told myself. "He is doing it again, wanting me to believe that he was sorry. Please, God, make this person just go away. Would I see him or hear his voice again?"

And then we were outside to face the media.

Reporters wanted to talk to me, get my reaction to the guilty pleas and sentencing. Was it fair?

There is nothing fair when you take someone's life. There is nothing fair when you are left with a hole in your heart. I had to move forward, knowing this part of my life was over and a new chapter was beginning.

Brian and Blaine are serving life sentences with no possibility of parole in separate Pennsylvania prisons.

Chapter 5

Wearing the Shoes of Grief

Simply put, children shouldn't die before their parents. When they lose a child, parents become part of a club they never asked to join. Members of the club share the feeling that they can't go on. They might feel that life is not worth living. One thing is certain: Life as they know it will never be the same.

They say grief comes in stages, but passing through the stages can't be rushed. There is no studying. No CliffsNotes. No Reader's Digest version. Grief is about coming to terms with the death of a child. For parents, not grieving is not an option. It is the hardest work they will ever do.

Grief comes with no rules. The stages come when they come. They go when they go. The grieving process takes time. How much time? Again, there are no rules or deadlines.

Everyone's journey is unique. Not everyone experiences all aspects of acute grief or each stage of grief. Grieving parents might move from one stage and end up returning. They might move forward and then go back. Visiting stages multiple times, going backwards, not going through a specific stage are all normal. Even years later, it is normal to re-visit one of the stages. There is no set time frame for each stage. There is no right or wrong way to grieve. A person's life experiences have a direct correlation to the grieving/mourning process. But all grieving parents need to be patient with themselves.

One basic rule: If a grieving parent wants to physically harm themselves or another person, they need to tell someone, a friend, family member or professional.

If a parent turns to a professional, they work as a team to navigate the grieving process.

> The psychologist Nancy saw the first year helped her work through the many decisions she had to make, but she cautioned Nancy that her extreme need to be in control would take its toll.
>
> Her prediction came true just days before the arrest of Blaine Norris. Nancy was taken from work to the hospital, and a few months later she fainted in a restaurant. Both times, doctors called what happened an anxiety attack. Eventually, Nancy was diagnosed with post-traumatic stress disorder.

In the first year, parents will unveil intimate details about who they are and exactly what their needs are in order to get through an hour, a day or a week. Details will emerge that the parents never knew about themselves. Parents will learn how to prepare for and predict what they will need and how they will react to certain people, events, pictures, items belonging to the loved one and more. They will learn to expect how long the reaction will last and what they need to do to take care of themselves. Reflecting on memories of the deceased child will be part of a parent's life-long journey. Memories will range from pleasant to extremely painful.

> Nancy couldn't bring herself to look at Randi's baby pictures for three years. It was important to her to see only the adult Randi, who had been so

brutally taken from her. Looking at photos of Randi grown up made Nancy feel her daughter was watching over her. For a year, everywhere Nancy went, she carried a photo of her daughter taken during their last Christmas together.

Today, pictures of Randi as an adult hang on her refrigerator. "I want to make sure that each morning when I wake up, I see her smiling face. I need to remember how happy she was," Nancy said.

Easy? No way. Friends, relatives and co-workers might suggest it's time to move on, to heal. They might note that life is full of difficulties, and all one needs is strength to overcome them.

Nancy's family suggested she remove all photos of Brian from her home. But where you saw Brian, you saw Randi. Nancy was tortured by the thought of removing Randi's wedding picture: Randi and Brian, an elegant bride and groom, posed on a set of swirling white steps in the Capitol complex.

Nancy recalled Randi's happiness that day. Mother and daughter called it the best day of their lives. Randi died without knowing she had married a monster.

Nancy realized that when she looked at the picture, her eyes went only to Randi. So the wedding picture hangs prominently in her house to this day.

Would it be the right decision for someone else? Maybe not. But it brings Nancy comfort, which is all that matters.

The process, anxiety and sadness, comprise a nightmare that never ends. There is no quick fix and no universal solution. But over time each nightmare will be a little less horrible than the one before. Slowly, ever so slowly, the grieving parent will develop tools to cope.

Acute grief: This comes in the days following the death. The parent will be unable to concentrate. He or she will find it impossible to read a document or newspaper as the lines blur or jump around. There is too much activity in the brain; thousands of images flash one after another. The images won't stop. They cannot be controlled. People will walk through the door. They will be familiar, but the parent might not remember their names.

Simple, everyday tasks and routines are not possible without significant concentration or help from others. Something as simple as getting dressed might take hours.

> Paul would say, "Lynn, it's time to get dressed."
> "Why," she would think, "do I need to get dressed? I have clothes on. They may be pajamas, but they are clothes."
> This simple task, something Lynn had done thousands of times before, now required directions.
> Paul would say, "Lynn, put your socks on."
> She would put on one and stare. Twenty minutes later, Paul would return and say, "Lynn, put on the other sock."
> It was a painstaking process.

Grieving parents often lose control over their emotions. The tears are unstoppable. Emotionally, there are bad days and worse days. Finding something that belonged to the child, a piece of clothing, a pillow, might stop the parent cold. If it holds the child's scent, the parent might not want to let it go.

> When Nancy took possession of Randi's house, she brought all of her daughter's belongings back to the home they had shared. "I fixed her room up just as it was when she was a little girl. I placed her hope chest by her bed, surrounded by her stuffed toys. I put all the dolls she had collected on shelves as they

once were. Going into her room makes me feel her presence," Nancy said.

Making a decision is all but impossible those first days. Yet parents are being asked about funeral services, what clothing to put on the child, what words to include in the obituary.

Making plans is almost as difficult. If a parent lacks the confidence that she can make it through the day, how can she commit to something in the future? A well-meaning request, such as a quiet lunch, makes the grieving parent feel anxious and overwhelmed.

If a parent says yes, the commitment might become an obsession. Every day the parent thinks of excuses and reasons to cancel, sometimes canceling on the day of the event.

It's simply too overwhelming. The mind asks, "What will I wear? How do I get there? What if I need to leave? Will people talk about my child? Will I lose it?"

It is not uncommon to cancel events a parent once enjoyed. The parent's mind dissects every moment, every possibility and turns what might be a simple event into something monumental. Some routine functions become overwhelming.

If parents do go out, they see their child everywhere. That's him across the street. That's her walking half a block ahead. They rush to catch up, only to face a stranger.

Parents might have no appetite. Often, they eat only because someone places food in front of them and orders them to eat. Physical ache accompanies a broken heart. The sadness and emptiness are overwhelming.

Lynn: "In the beginning, I would tell people that I wasn't going to make it, but I couldn't explain what I meant by that. I experienced a physical heaviness on my chest. I jumped at the slightest noise. I couldn't be alone. In hindsight, I was afraid that I was going to lose my mind and need to be committed."

Parents might have difficulty in sleeping, or might sleep for hours on end. Lynn would have slept the day away if Paul wasn't there to keep her moving. Nancy could fall asleep without any warning, even while sitting at a traffic light or in a meeting at work.

Parents might think they are crazy. They are not. This is all normal, exhausting, hard work, and part of the grieving process.

Shock/numbness: Often, the first uncontrollable stage is shock or numbness. It is impossible for parents to prepare for the murder of their child. Their first reaction is total disbelief, and they lose any sense of normalcy or control. They might feel as though the wind has been knocked out of them, that they have been hit by a truck.

Fortunately, the body is able to determine how much physical and emotional suffering it can endure. When parents have reached their limit, the body has a way of screaming, "Enough." It will shut down. Parents might find themselves unable to walk, think, feel, cry, hear or talk coherently. It is also normal for some people to scream, run or attack.

Parents can function, but might act as though they are in a stupor. They can follow directions, but they must be detailed. Outsiders have no clue how difficult everyday life can be. Parents rarely share the details of how they feel. Why would they? They already feel inadequate, hopeless and useless.

It is normal for grieving parents to walk toward the kitchen or bathroom, then forget why they are walking. Similarly, it is normal to misplace items and search for hours, only to forget what the search was for.

When the body is ready, it will begin to let the reality in. This stage might take days or weeks. As the shock and numbness diminish, the loss of the child begins to become more real, and often the parent begins to go through the next stage, denial.

Denial: This is a way to slow the inevitable, the pain and the realization that a child is gone. Parents are slow to accept the loss. Denial often walks hand-in-hand with shock. The parent is convinced that the child will walk through the door. The parent's mind says the child is out with friends or on a vacation and will return shortly. The phone rings, and parents expect to hear the child's voice on the other end.

> Nancy: "I would sit by the phone at work and wait for Randi's daily telephone call each morning. I would wait to hear from Randi on the way home from work, when she would chat about her day or plans for dinner."

Denial is the body's way of delaying. The parent is stuck in the foreword of a book and unwilling to start Chapter 1. Denial might last hours, days or weeks.

In both shock and denial, parents experience mostly negative feelings. What happens when a positive feeling enters and the parent smiles? Someone offers a hug, and the parent feels safe in the embrace. Someone shares a memory of the child, and the parent laughs out loud.

Guilt comes on the heels of the smile. Guilt, guilt and more guilt. Parents beat themselves up because they cannot understand how it can be possible to feel anything good.

Guilt/bargaining: Bargaining is most common in those instances in which a loved one is clinging to life. "Dear God," the parent prays, "if you save my child, I promise I will do (something, anything)." Parents beat themselves up. They ask, "Why didn't I see this coming?" They say, "If only I had done this, then the unthinkable wouldn't have happened." They recall, "My child wanted me to do something with them and I was busy taking care of life."

Parents' heads are filled with "I should have" and "What if?" They feel like failures. Parents are supposed to protect their children, regardless of their age or circumstances. They offer up prayers. "Please, God, let this be a mistake. Please let this be a dream. Let me wake up from this nightmare and find everything back to normal."

The only things normal are the parents' thoughts. The guilt and bargaining are a stage, an effort to delay the truth from settling in. The child is dead.

> Nancy: "Guilt is my greatest burden. Was I too conservative with my money? Did I deprive Randi of materialistic things? Did she always want more?"

Nancy wonders if she should have demanded more child support, if she was too strict, if she should have remarried and given Randi a brother or sister. When Randi met Brian, should Nancy have asked more questions, interrogated his family?

Despite her feelings of guilt, in her heart of hearts, Nancy knows she carries no responsibility. "I think that Brian wanted Randi dead, that nothing could have stopped him," she said.

Lynn's guilt over her inability to protect her children clung to her for many years. In 2005, she said, her nephew Bob had his first child. Two weeks after the birth, Bob and his wife wanted to go to a wedding, so they asked Lynn to watch the baby, who was known to the family as A.J.

"The day arrived and something was wrong with me," Lynn said. "I went to the grocery store to pick up a few items and had a panic attack in Aisle Three.

"I made it home and realized that I was scared to death to be alone watching a baby. How could anyone trust me with their child when I couldn't even protect my own? When they arrived, I broke down sobbing and told them I didn't think I could do it. I didn't know how to take care of a baby. I couldn't take care of Jen and Dave, so I asked, 'Why are you trusting me with your son?'

"My nephew and his wife should have grabbed that baby, ran and called the psych ward for a pick up. Instead, he gave me a big hug. He told me I was a wonderful mom to Jen and Dave. They loved me; they trusted me completely to watch A.J. He handed me the baby and walked out the door. I held and stared at that baby for hours. I was just fine."

Anger: When children are murdered, parents, naturally, are angry at the person who killed them. But their anger also may be directed at people trying to help them. Anger grows because the parent is powerless and couldn't control the situation, couldn't prevent the murder from happening.

In her dreams, Lynn killed Tom repeatedly in every bloody, violent way. Nancy dreamed of sitting in a prison watching the state inject needles into the arms of Brian and Blaine.

But parents also experience a secondary anger directed at themselves. Anger and guilt can stick together. Parents are very good at blaming themselves for not doing their job of protecting their children. They also are angry because they will replay every moment they spent or didn't spend with the child and beat themselves up over every lost moment.

Lynn: "Why did I clean instead of go outside and play? Why did I spend an hour on the phone with a friend instead of reading them a book or playing a game? Why didn't I let them have the dog they wanted? Why did I give David so many time-outs? Why did I send them to their rooms or make them clean their rooms? David loved Monopoly and Jen loved crafts. Why didn't I spend more time doing what they enjoyed? Could I have told them more often how much I loved them?"

Parents poke at what they perceive as faults until they wind up feeling like a slice of Swiss cheese.

The anger directed at people trying to help might have its roots in envy or disbelief. Their lives are normal. The parents' can never be. Don't they understand that your child has died? How can their lives go forward?

These thoughts are normal and all part of the process.

Still, guilt and anger can be dangerous. Parents blame themselves and want to punish themselves, thinking they should have done something differently.

> Nancy: "Why did I go on that cruise? If I had been home, Brian would never have gone ahead with his plot. He wouldn't have had the nerve if he thought I might drop in at any time."

If Brian, Blaine and Tom really wanted to kill Randi, Jen and Dave, could they have done it even if Nancy and Lynn had completed all of their "if only's?" The answer is most likely yes. It's really important to step back and evaluate the situation. If the guilt and blame become overwhelming, it is time to turn to a professional. It's important for the parent to be able to evaluate the situation and determine if she is creating an unrealistic scenario and exaggerating her role in what has occurred.

> Guilt and blame overwhelmed Lynn. Paul saw it. So he set up an appointment with Jeff Verrecchio, a psychologist in Camp Hill, whose door has remained open to Lynn for 19 years. When Lynn walked into his office the first time, she was catatonic, devastated. It took years of Lynn talking and Jeff listening for Lynn to arrive where she is today.
>
> Jeff credits Lynn's underlying strong personality for getting her through those years. And he credits Paul.
>
> "Paul," he said, "offers a model of what to do." Paul listened to Lynn for hours on end, but never offered advice or solutions unless asked.

Acceptance: The word does not mean that parents are okay or are finished grieving. Instead, they have reached a stage in which they are able to accept the reality that the child is dead. From here, the parent might bounce between the stages of grief.

The bereaved parent is about to build a new life. Regardless of how much love, care and support are provided by friends and family, the parents will need to dig deeper than they ever thought possible. What lies ahead is tough work, as parents determine what their future will hold. They have to feel the pain and sadness. To bottle those feelings and try to be stoic can greatly impact health, mentally and physically.

Depression: This is the most common emotion after the death of child. Sadness and depression last the longest, are usually associated with every stage, and might include a lifetime of mourning. The parent has fallen to the bottom of the barrel and might feel like she is trying to climb a ladder without rungs. Parents might begin to disengage from others. They might feel the answer lies with isolation. Parents really struggle with thoughts of how to go forward without their child. Their lives will be forever changed. It is not uncommon to become obsessed with the mortality of others, as well as your own.

> Lynn: "I had a Sunday morning ritual for years. I would need to read every single obituary. I wanted to see how many people died who were close to my age, Paul's age, were children or were close to my parents' age. I became obsessed with dying. In fact, each time I got on a plane, I prayed before and during the flight that the plane would crash.
>
> "My husband, Paul, wasn't too thrilled with my prayers as he sat in the seat next to me. I just wanted to be with Jen and Dave, and if my life was cut short by an accident or illness, that would be a blessing. I was ready."

Depression is normal in a person trying to cope with the loss. Severe or prolonged depression that includes thoughts of suicide, not sleeping or sleeping too much, loss of interests once enjoyed, significant change in diet, withdrawal from others, or a feeling that you have nothing to live for may indicate the need to talk with a professional.

> Nancy: "At one time, I thought about taking my life. Driving home from a memorial at Hershey Medical Center, I just felt so alone. I wanted to die and be with Randi. A tractor-trailer came up behind me and I slowed down. He honked his horn and took me out of that state of mind."

Mourning: This is the journey one takes for the rest of his or her life. How do you accept that your children are no longer a part of your life? How do you build a life without them, yet keep them alive in your heart and mind? In the beginning, after the death, parents might feel as though they are operating in a world of black and white. Then one day they will notice a flower that is no longer black and white. Suddenly, there is color! Seeing color is a good sign that the bereaved is working hard and making progress. A parent might still feel uncertain that she can live with the loss, but the lens has changed ever so slightly.

> Nancy: "There is a cardinal that comes each spring and sits on the back deck. Each time I see that cardinal, I think of Randi and know that she is looking after me.
> "Randi is buried beside my father. When I visit Randi's grave, I sit on a bench. One day I recall seeing several yellow butterflies. I immediately thought how my dad loved the color yellow. Then I remembered a story I read about releasing a butterfly to symbolize releasing your child into God's hands.

"A friend released 25 butterflies at Randi's wedding. Each time I see butterflies, I think of Randi."

Chapter 6

A Glimpse of the Journey

After the funeral, the flowers, the solemn words, most mourners return to their routine. For the mother of a murder victim, nothing will ever be routine again.

For Lynn Shiner, Jennifer and David would be forever 10 and 8. There would be no more softball or baseball, no school concerts, no report cards, no sleepovers. The future held no birthday parties, driving lessons, graduations, weddings or grandchildren.

Nancy Chavez would have no grandchildren, either. She had lost her daughter, her best friend, her confidant. All that surrounded her was fear. Someone had brutally murdered her daughter. No one knew why, and Nancy could only think that whoever it was would be coming for her next.

Lynn and Nancy both work for the state of Pennsylvania. They buried their children, and in about two weeks, they returned to their jobs. By some standards, that's generous leave time. Somehow society has gotten the idea that a parent whose child has been murdered will be clear-headed enough to return to work in 14 days or less.

Nancy was there physically. Her mind, however, focused on Randi.

"Nothing else but Randi's murder mattered to me when I returned to work two weeks after Randi was killed," Nancy said. "My work was always my life, as I knew that it provided support for Randi and me. My colleagues became part of my extended family. Anyone who knew me also knew Randi, although they may have never met her. When I returned to work, I was very sensitive to how Randi's murder impacted them. Their avoidance was not unexpected."

In early 2003, Pennsylvania had a new governor, and Nancy's job was in jeopardy. With the help of her boss and Greg, who was director of human services, she was fortunate to be transferred. She moved into a new job and a new department. At least it was in familiar territory; she had worked there before.

In Nancy's absence, as in Lynn's, the state had sent in help. The Keystone Crisis Intervention Team spoke with Nancy's co-workers. The State Employee Assistance Program counseled Lynn's co-workers in the Department of Labor and Industry. In those sessions, employees were able to speak about the murders and their feelings and receive advice on how to deal with their grieving co-workers upon their return.

When Lynn returned, she admits she was a useless employee for months. Jim, her boss, told her, "You have a lot of co-workers who will do anything for you; just ask. If you can't work, it's okay, just sit there."

Nancy heard from her bosses early on.

"I remember how Sheri Phillips (then deputy secretary for the Department of General Services) and Kelly Logan (secretary of DGS) called me at home that first day," Nancy said. "Sherri came to my house and assured me not to worry about work. I should take as much time as I needed. Honestly, I could not think of work or returning to work. That was the furthest thought from my mind."

Work? How can we expect anyone to work so shortly after a horrifying trauma?

"My life was in a blur the first two years," Nancy said. "I look back now and know from the words I wrote in my journal and friends sharing our discussions in 2003 and 2004 that I was in shock. I lived each day with so much anxiety. My attention span was short. I jumped from one issue to the next, especially in that first year. The first two years I had no control of my body, and anxiety would consume me. My body would shake, my fingers would get numb and I would feel tightness in my chest. I felt that I was having a heart attack.

"In the first two years, I could not focus on anything specific other than Randi's murder," Nancy said. "That was tough for me, as I have always been driven to set goals and have time lines to complete projects. For two years, I could not read a novel other than crime stories. I felt that I needed to know how homicides were solved or why people kill.

"I could not work on my crafts that I always did on a daily basis. I had always been driven by making something special for Randi, crocheting a blanket, knitting sweaters or working on a cross-stitch project. I just had no ambition to do anything. I had no desire to exercise. What value did it have to me? I did not need to lose weight, as I had lost so much and had little strength. I realized later how much my exercise helped me emotionally. It gave me purpose and a time to support a healthy mind."

"My expectations of myself were always so high. I remember thinking over and over, 'Get control of your life.' I could not let Randi down now. I could not let my family down. My friend Vicki never knew how much she helped me through this crisis. She pushed me to go to the YMCA at lunch each day, as we had done previously.

"In 2003, I saw my relationship with Greg had changed. Prior to that, we had gone out on a few dates, nothing more. From the moment I learned that he had been in the meditation room at the airport, I knew that he was special. He never left my side from that moment on. He was at the funeral and stayed with me many days and nights. I could see that I needed him more than ever. He made me feel safe, comforted me, and listened to me talk continuously about Randi.

"Ironically, for so many years, I did not have a man in my life. That was my choice. My father and brother-in-law had been mentors to Randi. Greg came into my life through work. I believe that it was Randi's murder that brought us closer together. I was so weak and vulnerable, and I cherished how he took me under his wing and protected me. He helped me to make the right decisions. He took me away from the chaos when I needed it. I always believed that Randi had something to do with this.

"I would say that after Brian and Blaine were incarcerated, I began to put my life back together. I worried that my family members would die and leave me alone. To this day, I worry about them leaving me alone."

Lynn spent the months after her children were murdered under the watchful eye of Paul. Lynn was standing on the edge of an abyss, and Paul was afraid, no he knew, she wanted to take a step and disappear into nothingness.

"My life was over," Lynn said. "I didn't want to live. I only wanted to be with Jen and Dave. I had nothing to live for. It's so hard to describe what I went through during the first few days and months. I really knew what it meant to have a broken heart. I felt like I had a 50-pound block on my chest, and thoughts of ending my life were frequent."

Paul was, by then, a member of the family. No piece of paper made that official. He put himself there and refused to budge. He moved Lynn into his house. He knew she wanted to die, so he made sure she was watched every minute of every day. He agreed that her parents should sell their home and move in with them. They still had a home in Florida, where they would stay for five months out of the year. Lynn, the youngest of her parents' four children, prayed daily to God, begging Him to let her parents survive for another decade. She simply didn't know if she could go on without them.

Lynn's father could see that.

"Bet (his wife) and me were scared for Lynn. The daughter we knew was no longer there, and we were afraid that she wasn't going to make it," he said.

Paul not only watched Lynn like a hawk, he cried with her, listened to her, held her. He found her a psychologist, drove her to the cemetery, prepared her meals, ran her errands, helped her decorate the children's grave on holidays, pushed her to stay physically active, and much more.

"Thank God for Paul. I'm pretty certain I would be dead without him," Lynn said. "I needed someone to talk to, to share all of my feelings and thoughts, regardless of how scattered or dark they were. I didn't need Paul to have the answers or know exactly what to say, but just to listen and validate that my feelings were normal, and somehow, with his love and support, I was going to be okay if we just took it day by day. Even when I had thoughts of suicide for the five-plus years, we made a pact that I would tell him I was having those thoughts and would share exactly what the thoughts were, including how I would do it. Being able to openly talk about suicide made the anxiety and thoughts associated with dying subside."

When Paul had to work, he left Lynn with Ruth and Leo Brown, a couple who had been babysitters, more like a second set of parents, to Jen and Dave when they were younger. Lynn was broken and fragile, so Ruth and Leo followed her lead. If she was tired, they let her sleep. If she wanted to talk about Jen and Dave, they listened. If she wanted to rant or cry, that was okay, too. They gave her what she needed.

On days when work was too much, she would retreat to Ruth and Leo's unannounced. Lynn would ring the doorbell, and receive a hug -- no questions asked. She would curl up on a couch, put her feet on the dog and fall asleep. All around her, on mattresses on the floor, lay sleeping young children from Ruth and Leo's day care home. Sometimes she would play games with the kids, or hold them on her lap on a swing, or chase them. It was an escape, being with the children. They didn't see the pain, just the love.

On the nights that Paul didn't work, he would make dinner, and then Lynn would begin her nightly ritual, which lasted for more than a year: She would soak in the tub on her stomach, staring at the faint black lines in the worn porcelain tub, and think of Jen and Dave and how they died. Jennifer had been killed while she slept, and everyone assured Lynn that

Jen's death had been instant, with no suffering. But David had left his bed and run to his father. Defensive wounds on his hands bore witness to his struggle to live. Now his mother was obsessed with David's final minutes, his confusion, his fear, his courage, and most of all, his thoughts of why his daddy would do this to him.

Her pain was so intense, Lynn said, that she expected to have a heart attack. She was filled with rage and hatred. Every night she and Paul punished themselves with questions. Why, what if, they asked over and over. The biggest question was why hadn't Tom Snead just killed himself? Why had he taken her beautiful, innocent children? Lynn and Paul had this discussion every single day. "Often times, we parroted the discussion from the hour or day before. It was simply a discussion that consumed us and became as routine as waking up or eating a meal," Lynn said.

In the beginning, Lynn had an overwhelming need for detail. She read newspaper articles over and over, memorizing every detail of her children's last minutes. She became obsessed with learning how other people had heard the news, what they had been doing at the time, how they had reacted and if they were okay.

Lynn requested and received the coroner's report about one month after her children died. "It sat on the dining room table for days as I readied myself for the details," she said. "As many mothers who have been in this situation can relate, regardless of how painful, I needed to know every single detail of Jen and Dave's murder." With Paul by her side, she opened the envelope. Unable to concentrate, and vision blurred from sobbing, Lynn had to read the report over and over until she understood every last detail.

"I was offered, but declined, the clothing they were wearing at the time of their deaths," Lynn said. "I know parents who have the unopened brown-paper-wrapped clothing, and I know other parents who opened, touched and smelled the clothing without any thought of the blood that the clothes were soaked in. These are normal, personal choices."

In the weeks and months that followed the funeral, Lynn began having panic attacks. She felt she was losing her mind. She would turn on a burner to make coffee and put the kettle on another burner. She would return home from work to find she had put the cereal in the refrigerator and left the milk on the counter all day. She had a panic attack because she couldn't boil water for spaghetti and heat the sauce at the same time. A simple task such as grocery shopping overwhelmed her.

"In a grocery store, I would have a panic attack because I didn't know how I would find everything I needed," she said. "When I got home, I would sit on the kitchen floor and cry because I didn't know how I was going to be able to put all the groceries away."

She recalls getting into her car and driving several feet, only to realize she hadn't removed the locking device from the steering wheel. She would see people who had been co-workers for 18 years and be unable to remember their names.

All the while images of Jen and Dave flashed through her mind 24/7. "It's hard to explain," Lynn said. "The images were constant and not one after another. Maybe 20 at a time overlapping the images that were already there." Even Lynn knew she was suicidal. She wondered, if Jen and Dave had died of knife wounds is that how she should end her life too? "I wouldn't touch a knife for over a year. I wouldn't even cut my own food because I was afraid I'd kill myself," Lynn said.

It fell to Paul to do most everything.

Nancy, too, describes flashing images and an obsession with knives.

"I have continuous thoughts about Randi's final minutes," she said. "I have recurring thoughts of Randi screaming when she was being strangled in the dark. It was not until 2006 that I had to ask questions. I remember asking the coroner if Randi suffered. How far did that knife go into her? What killed her? Was it true when Blaine said that Randi was praying when he was stabbing her? Was this all true? I got to know Mike Norris, the coroner. He sat me down and answered the questions."

Nancy warns that what she recalls might not be accurate. "My memories are based on the recurring flashbacks of what I experienced or what I heard. I do not remember walking out of the airport with my family and vaguely remember being at the cemetery. I do remember picking up the phone at 12:15 p.m. on Monday, January 13, 2003, and the coroner saying, 'The deceased died of multiple stab wounds and strangulation.' I don't remember if I fell to my knees or just dropped the phone. That was the first time I learned how she was killed.

"What occurred was more of a blur. I cope with my flashbacks of hearing the coroner say in the preliminary hearing that the knife that killed Randi was six inches long. I see that knife with her blood. On a recurring basis, I see Randi lying in her garage or her standing at her front door waving bye to me, or hearing her cry as I talked from a pay phone at Phillipsburg, St. Maarten telling me that she missed and loved me.

"One of my biggest challenges is to remember. The first years I protected myself from reading any papers or seeing any pictures of the crime scene for fear of dealing with the trauma. My brother-in-law Mike warned me he saw a few of the photos and told me under no circumstances would I ever want to see them. He will never get those images out of his mind."

But Nancy had to deal with a double whammy. After the loss of Randi came the discovery that Randi's husband had plotted her murder.

"I was devastated," Nancy recalled. "I couldn't even think why he would want to kill her. It didn't make sense to me. To think that I sat with him, I hugged him, I did everything for him, and he betrayed me."

Keeping the secret of Brian's involvement while police prepared their case churned her up inside. "For four solid months, I had to live a lie. Each time I talked to Brian, I had to make him believe I knew nothing. I couldn't reveal it. I couldn't say anything. I felt I was betraying my family by not telling them," Nancy said. "It was horrible, absolutely horrible. I could not talk about it to anyone. … I had to treat Brian as normal."

Nancy knew the police were tailing Brian, watching his movements and his friends. Nancy was left being betrayed, humiliated and scared. "I became very fearful of him and what he might do to me. I recorded every conversation I had with him and felt nauseated just hearing him talk about how much he loved Randi."

And what about the actual killer? Would he come after her? In Nancy's dreams, people chased her. She dreamed of being killed by a shotgun blast.

For the first year after Randi's death, Nancy wanted to shut everyone out. "I didn't want people to know I was not able to cope," she said.

Nancy had feared bullies all her life. As a child, she had been harassed because she was Mexican. As a young woman, she had been abused by her husband. Now, her daughter's husband had turned out to be the worst kind of bully of all.

For two years after Randi's murder, she said, "I would not go out of my house without having someone with me. I would not go out in public places. I was afraid that people would be talking about me and point their finger, saying, 'She is the woman who just lost her daughter.' I was afraid that the media would see me and want to talk to me.

"Greg and Linda Morrison took me to a car show in the fall of 2003. They thought that getting me out of the house would help me. I clung onto Greg's arm with the fear of him leaving me alone. I came out of the restroom and could not find them, as they had drifted off looking at a car nearby. I panicked, walking around and around the cars. They found me, not knowing how this affected me."

In her fear, she had new locks put on her doors and motion lights installed on every end of the house. "Randi's murder created a new level of fear," she said. "From day one I was afraid of walking into my garage without the light on. I fear the dark now and think I see someone. Every time I look at my dashboard before I pull out of my garage, it says, 'check surrounding area.' I think of someone waiting for me in the garage. When I open my garage, I pause before I pull in and look to see if someone is waiting for me, as Randi's killer did.

"Gardening, sitting outside or taking a walk in the neighborhood were always so much pleasure for me. It took almost two years before I could do those again alone."

Nancy, who had viewed herself as a strong woman who had left an abusive husband, raised a strong and beautiful daughter and educated them both, felt powerless. All control of her life had been snatched away by a coward.

She saw a psychologist for a time, but refused any form of medication. It was as if she wanted to feel all her pain, Greg said.

Lynn went through intense therapy and used no medicine for the first eight months. She simply let Jeff guide her through many of the stages of grief. As her thoughts of suicide became stronger, she was placed on an anti-depressant.

When Nancy's sister Linda gave birth to a baby girl six months after Randi's death, it was a bittersweet moment. "Going to the hospital to see her just tore me apart. I thought about holding Randi. It just brought back memories."

Seeing other people with young children, or grandparents with their grandchildren, was painful. With her only child gone, Nancy knew she would never experience that joy.

All types of joyful occasions can serve as painful reminders for a parent who has lost a child.

A year or two after her children were murdered, Lynn agreed to go with Paul to his niece's wedding.

"I felt fine," Lynn said. "Then, as she walked down that aisle, it hit me; all I could see was Jennifer's face. The front of my blouse was soaked with my tears. To know that I would never see my daughter experience that joy took me back to the beginning, and I felt all of the pain and emotion that was associated with their murder. Each wedding thereafter, the pain and sadness lightened, and I could feel happiness for the person being married."

After the murders, Lynn vowed she would never celebrate Christmas again. How could she be festive on the anniversary of her children's deaths?

Lynn's sister, also named Nancy, and a friend went to Lynn's house after the murders, dismantled her Christmas tree, unwrapped the gifts intended for Jen and Dave, and returned them. "Later, I went through the decorations and kept a single shoe box full, the ones made by Jen and Dave. Jen and I had begun collecting Santas, and I gave those to Ruth and Leo. Everything else, wreaths, ornaments, lights, stockings, down to Christmas music, went to Goodwill. I was done with Christmas," Lynn said.

"For 10 years, "I just couldn't function well the entire month of December."

But Christmas went on without her, and people tried to pull her in. "Over the years, my family, friends and co-workers continued to engage me at Christmastime," Lynn said. "It seemed no one could understand. Why would I ever celebrate the day my children were murdered? People wanted normal back, and I wasn't having anything to do with it. For those who still chose to give me presents, I never reciprocated. I would take them home and Paul would open them. I couldn't even touch the paper. I know now that they cared and wanted to share a gift with me. Then, I could only think, 'I've told everyone that I don't want anything to do with Christmas. How cruel to give me a gift to remind me of the loss of Jen and Dave and what they will never have.'"

In 1996, Lynn took a baby step: She bought a small Christmas tree and decorated it with 100 angels that family and friends had given her in memory of Jen and Dave.

Then, in 2002, Lynn's father began laying on the guilt. He said he didn't know how many Christmases he had left, but he really wanted to have at least one with all his family together.

"I really struggled," Lynn said. "I still wanted nothing to do with Christmas, yet my parents had been so good to me. I didn't want to deny 'a dying man's wish.' So I agreed to Christmas dinner at our house, but just dinner and family time, absolutely no presents."

For the occasion, Lynn added a second Christmas tree. The first had purple lights for Jen and was adorned with angels, and the other was decked out in red lights for Dave and loaded with snowmen. Lynn's dad wanted to put Christmas lights on the outside of the house, so she let him. They were purple, red and gold. Until then, Lynn figured people in the neighborhood probably thought the house was owned by a Jewish family because it had been dark at Christmas for years.

With the decorations in place, Lynn began praying for snow. She wanted enough snow to keep everyone at home.

"We got up early and we had about a half inch of freezing ice on the ground. Snow had begun to fall as I walked out to get the newspaper. In the middle of the driveway, on top of the ice, there were initials formed in snow that resembled the letters 'DS.' David Snead. In my mind, David was letting me know that it was okay to celebrate Christmas."

It continued to snow, but Lynn's family arrived anyway, and they shared a quiet Christmas dinner together.

In 2003, Paul and Lynn exchanged presents, and the following year they gave gifts to family and friends. In 2006, they began a tradition. Each Christmas Eve they invite 15 or 20 family and friends for a Christmas Eve dinner of Italian food and homemade desserts. "We call it 'no carb left behind,'" Lynn joked. "It has become a wonderful, loving time to express how much those who join us mean to us and to remember and honor Jen and Dave."

Nancy also avoided holidays, particularly Christmas, in the early years after Randi's death.

"Holidays were never the same," Nancy said. "I could not put up a Christmas tree for almost three years. My friends coaxed me and begged to help me. I just could not see putting up a tree and celebrating a holiday that Randi loved so much without her. I did not want to relive the pain of taking the Christmas tree down in her house and packing the beautiful ornaments away forever.

"Putting up a tree would never be the same. We would put on Christmas music, and Randi would reminisce about where she got each ornament she placed on the tree. It took us hours," Nancy recalled.

But Christmas is not the only holiday a grieving parent has to survive. The calendar is filled with special events that can make a rough journey even bumpier. April was a cruel month for Lynn, because both Jennifer and David had been born in April, Lynn's bookends to tax day. Lynn also had problems with back-to-school advertisements, school buses and Halloween, her children's second-favorite holiday. And then there was Mother's Day to get through.

Lynn compares an approaching birthday or holiday to a roller-coast ride. First comes the climb. Then the day arrives and she finds herself sitting atop the coaster ready to descend. Finally, there's the actual ride, getting through the day.

The climb is filled with anticipation; she's holding on to the bar with white knuckles, not knowing how difficult the day will be. She's filled with memories, loss, disorientation and the overriding desire to make the event or holiday cease to exist. She doesn't want to participate. She just wants it to be over.

On the actual day, when she's sitting at the top of the roller coaster, she must go through the motions. She puts on a face, but the pain and sadness surround her as she endures the day. As the day passes, she thinks about all that's occurred, her feelings and sadness, but she feels some relief. She didn't think she would make it, but she did.

Anticipation, the days or weeks before the holiday, is the hardest part, Lynn said. But the cliché is somewhat correct: Time heals all wounds, or, at least, dulls them. After 19 years, she said, "the roller coaster hasn't gone away for me. In my mind, I have it down; I know what the ride is like. Some events have faded and have little impact, but birthdays and Christmas are tough. The mind tries to help you through the logic. You know the routine; you'll be ok; you know that your loved one would want you to be happy, but the heart simply doesn't always listen to the mind. And that's ok. I've learned to simply accept the ride.

"After a while," she said, "you learn you're going to come back out of it and you deal with it."

A defining moment came in 2008, with the death of Lynn's mother, who had been diagnosed with small cell lung cancer the previous year. "She was one of the strongest women I ever knew and wasn't ready to die," Lynn said. "She never complained and did the chemotherapy and radiation until her body said, 'no more.'

"She was my rock. She would do anything for her children. A woman with a tough exterior and a heart of gold."

Lynn grieved as she watched her mother slowly fade away, with her father taking care of her mother's every need. "Paul and I tried to make her days as easy as possible," Lynn said. "I cut her hair off before it fell out, we played a lot of Scrabble, we bought her every single Shirley Temple movie we could find and we talked a lot about the kids. I told her everything I wanted her to tell the kids.

"It took seven months from diagnosis to death. We kept her at home as long as possible, but towards the end we wanted her to have the best of care and placed her in a nearby hospice home. For me, personally, I wasn't okay with her dying in our home, and I saw the toll it was beginning to take on my father. I didn't want to be her nurse in the end, just her daughter.

"Two days before my mom died, I told her that it was okay to go and that Jen and Dave were waiting for her. The next day, all of her family was there. Paul and I went home that night, and that was the night she died. An incredible sense of peace surrounded me knowing Jen and Dave would have their 'pistol-packing' grandmother. I was sad, but the peace and happiness I felt for Jen and Dave outweighed my sadness."

In Lynn's mind, there is no greater love than that of a mother. No matter how old she was, when something bad happened or she wasn't feeling well, she always wanted her mom. Even in the end, when her mother couldn't communicate, Lynn knew she understood what she was saying through her eyes. "When my mom died, a piece of my heart was taken, and at 47, the child in me also died. I didn't dwell on what I lost; I tried to treasure everything she had given me over my lifetime that will sustain me. Her death only means she is no longer here physically. She will always be my mom and I her daughter, and she will always be a part of me. My mom never asked for anything in life, but several months before she died, she asked that I take good care of my father. She didn't need to ask. Paul and I have done our best to do just that. He, too, is a very important person in our life. Without a doubt, my strength comes from my parents."

Death comes to all of us, but for a parent who has lost her only child, the future can be filled with chilling questions she might not want to answer.

"I have met with two financial advisers over the last year," Nancy said. "I go through a lot of pain thinking about planning for my future without Randi. I always planned my life based on Randi's goals. She wanted to be married at 25 and have two children in her early thirties. Now that she is not here, I cannot think of being alone. I live with the fear of being placed in a home and no one to take care of me.

"You would think Randi's death would have prompted me to write a will, get long-term care insurance and arrange my burial. I just can't. I have said year after year that this is the year that I will do it. I know I need to take the step, but I don't want to think about my assets, things Randi and I bought together on a shoestring, or keepsakes I cherish. I will never have grandchildren."

Like many people who have lost a loved one, Lynn is convinced that her children's spirits remain nearby. "From the very beginning," Lynn said, "I have always felt their presence," Lynn said. "The signs from the kids were constant.

"Two days before I returned to work, I thought it would be best if I met with several key staff from my work (Jim, Chuck, Karen and Denise) to provide details and answer questions about Jen and Dave's murder. The plan was they would meet with staff and share that information. We met at The Arches restaurant on Front Street.

"At one point in the conversation, I was talking about Christmas Eve day and shared the part where Jen came back in the house several times forgetting things. I got to the part where she came back in for the third time, and I asked her what she had forgotten this time. When I told them that she said she forgot to tell me how much she loved me, in that exact moment the lights in the restaurant went out. Not a flicker, out for about 10 seconds.

"Two minutes later, I was talking about David and his tight pants from eating too many cookies, and the lights went out again. My colleagues were speechless, and I believe it was Chuck who said something to the effect, 'Lynn, I think the kids are still with us.'"

Lynn had to agree.

"Within the first month of their death, I was sleeping, and I was awoken by a presence in the bedroom," Lynn said. "Jennifer was standing at the foot of the bed. I thought I was dreaming, but I wasn't. I sat up and motioned her over to the side of the bed and picked her up, light as a feather, and lay down with my arms around her, and slept holding her tight. People can say what they want. I am certain that was a real moment. Jennifer came back to hold and comfort her mom in all of her pain."

Another time, she lost the picture of Jen and Dave that was inside her locket. Lynn searched for days, and simply could not find it. "One day, I came home from work and the picture was laying in the middle of the foyer, their faces looking right at me. There is no way I walked over that picture every time I came down the stairs or through the front door for several days," Lynn said.

Paul and Lynn had a light in the living room that was on a timer to go on at dusk. On several occasions, they came home to find the light that was on the timer off, and a different light in the room on.

On Valentine's Day 1995, Lynn got out of bed and saw something on the floor next to her bed. It turned out to be a sticker with a heart and an angel on it. That sticker had been inside Jen's jewelry box, which was stored on the third floor of Paul's house. No one could explain how it came to be next to the bed.

Around the same time, Paul took Lynn to an area ski resort. They got on the chair lift and Paul pointed to the cushion next to Lynn's leg. Water had dropped from the bar overhead and formed a perfect smiley face next to her leg. There wasn't a drop of water anywhere else on the seat. A sign from David.

In 1997, Lynn went to see a medium. Years later, a woman she knew at work went to the same medium, although neither mentioned the other.

The medium told Lynn's co-worker, "There are a brother and sister standing here. They said that they were murdered by their father and that you are their mommy's friend. They said to please tell their mommy that they are okay and watching over her. Also, the brother said that he is taking care of his sister and then the sister said no she is taking care of their brother." Soon the children were arguing over who was taking care of whom.

The medium had a bracelet on, and the little boy said his mother would like that bracelet and that he wished he could give it to her for Mother's Day. The little girl said, "Please give my mommy two roses from me for Mother's Day."

The medium took off the bracelet and gave it to Lynn's co-worker. She asked if the co-worker knew who the children were, and the co-worker said yes. Then the medium asked the co-worker to give the bracelet to the children's mother.

In all, Lynn said, she has received more than 100 signs that her children are nearby.

Nancy also is convinced that Randi remains nearby.

"Over the years, I have seen Randi in my house," she said. "When I tell others, they look at me strangely. This has brought me comfort in my home.

"The first time, the night that I came home from the cruise, I laid in bed and saw her. She was an angel with beautiful white wings. She opened them and said, 'Mom, I am okay. I will look over you and protect you forever.'

"Other times, a light in her room has gone on during the night. I know that she is here. On another occasion, Greg woke up during the night and saw a shadow in her room. He came to me and told me.

"My house is full of angels, pins and ornaments that bring me the comfort that Randi is here with me. I wear her clothes at times. I was able to recover some of her jewelry and found a medal of the Virgin Mary and a heart that she wore. I wear that each day; I never take it off. I know that she is always with me," Nancy said.

Lynn describes the first year after losing a child as an overwhelming, devastating, emotional, painful, heartbreaking time. Yet, she said, "When I talk with others who have lost children, we all agree in hindsight, the first year was not the hard part. And trust us -- that was hard. Years two and three are when reality actually begins to set in. The shock wears off, changing of the guard occurs where old friends leave and new bonds are forged. The mind slowly begins to think more clearly, reality begins to set in, the numbness is fading, and you do everything possible to not have any idle time."

Lynn advises grieving parents to learn exactly what they need physically, emotionally and spiritually.

"I had many fears that I became obsessed with," she said. "My parents dying; Paul being in an accident; I was afraid of the dark; I was afraid to drive; I was obsessed with doors being locked, windows closed and locked. I couldn't sit still; I couldn't watch any television or movies that had any violence. I also was fearful of my future. To try to explain… Everyone has a book. Many of us have the same basic elements of a story: childhood good or bad, school, first car, marriage, kids, then grandkids, etc. Everyone has the same book with a few variations. But if you asked me to finish this book in 1994, I couldn't have finished the book. I was paralyzed with fear, as I couldn't imagine what kind of future I would have without Jen and Dave in my life.

"The only constant in my life was my job. My children had been murdered; I was no longer a parent; I lost my home; I moved in with Paul and now our relationship was on a completely different level. My safe, comfort and normal was gone.

Lynn married Tom despite a warning from a pastor who counseled them and despite her own feeling that something was not right about their union.

Lynn's babies, Jennifer, 2 and a half, and David, 6 months, peer out from under her bed.

David, pictured here at age three, loved snack foods. His last moments with his mother were spent laughing while she tried to button a pair of pants that had become too small for his growing body.

Jennifer at five. She would grow into a child who always aimed to please. She earned A's in school, loved to draw and played the clarinet.

Attached at the hip, Jennifer and her best friend Shannon Wood spent hours together.

These photos of the children were taken shortly before their murders. They were retrieved from a roll of film a police officer found in Tom Snead's camera after he murdered the children and killed himself.

Tom Snead's house, with his car parked in the driveway. When Lynn arrived there with Paul on Christmas morning, she looked in the sliding glass door on the right and saw Tom dead on the couch.

Lynn is always delighted to find flowers, balloons and tributes on Jen and Dave's grave. Their last name is not engraved on their headstone because Lynn couldn't bear to have them associated with their father.

In her grief, Lynn would often retreat to Ruth and Leo's daycare to find solace with the children.

Lynn and Pa. state Sen. Jeffrey Piccola at a news conference introducing the bill that would become Jen and Dave's law. (February 1996)

Lynn with Gov. Tom Ridge at a public signing of Jen and Dave's law in October of 1996.

Pastor Pat Wirick officiates the marriage of Paul and Lynn on the bank of the Susquehanna River in 1997.

Lynn and Paul attend one of the five Jen & Dave golf tournaments, which raised more than $160,000 for the fight against domestic violence.

After Lynn agreed to Christmas dinner at her house in 2002 she prayed for snow to keep everyone away. That morning she found her son's initials, "DS," on top of the ice in the driveway, a sign to Lynn that it was ok to celebrate the holiday.

Lynn accepts the National Crime Victims' Service Award from Attorney General John Ashcroft during a presentation in Washington, D.C. in April, 2004. With them is Assistant Attorney General, Deborah Daniels.

Lynn's parents, Ed and Betty Monk accompanied her to Washington for the award ceremony. Her mother was so proud she told everyone on the train and at a McDonald's of her daughter's accomplishments.

Nancy enjoyed taking Randi, pictured here in 1975 at 4 months, on daily walks to the beach at Ocean View Norfolk, Va.

Randi celebrated her fifth birthday with Nancy's family. Her favorite gift was the Miss Piggy doll.

Randi and Brian on their first date in 1995 at Hersheypark. As a child, Randi loved riding roller coasters and carousels.

Nancy's sister, Linda, and her husband Mike Wilson pause on the boardwalk in Ocean City, Md. in July 1996. The beach excursions were an annual event for family and friends.

Linda Morrison was known as the queen of volunteering at community events. She is pictured here with Nancy at the annual Back Yard Bash in July 1999.

Randi, the first grandchild, spent a lot of time with Nancy's parents. She posed for a picture with her Nana after getting her hair done.

Randi and Brian were married on September 9, 2000.
Photo courtesy of Picture Perfect Productions

Randi wanted a perfect wedding that included, from left to right, Gabriella Camplese, the maid of honor; her Aunt Linda Wilson, matron of honor; and bridesmaids Jill Berry and Cara Long.
Photo courtesy of Picture Perfect Productions

Randi bought the house at 221 Wood St. before she was married. The house, just three blocks from her mother's, was the scene of her murder.

Nancy and Randi on vacation at Ocean City, July 2001. Their best times were spent walking on the beach, wading in the water and talking about life.

Christmas was Randi's favorite holiday, and she loved having her family together to celebrate. This photo was taken on what would be her last Christmas in 2002.

Brian Trimble and Blaine Norris booking photos, 2003.

Randi's Race: A 5K Run/Walk for Hope and Courage is an annual fundraising event honoring Randi and all victims of domestic violence. This photo was taken on May 13, 2006.

Nancy and Greg visited Hawaii in July 2007.

Nancy accepted the Direct Energy and The Patriot News Harrisburg Volunteer of the Year Award at the Capitol Rotunda in May 2012.

Nancy's best friends and her support system, Deb Donahue and Samantha Krepps, attended the event at the Capitol in May 2012.

"Almost immediately, I became obsessed with routine and control. I needed eight hours of sleep or I became very emotional. I did nothing on the 'spur of the moment.' I knew exactly what I needed to make it through the day, down to knowing exactly how much gum I would chew.

For 10 years, Lynn slept with David's white stuffed dog and Jennifer's bunny. Even on trips, the dog and bunny were Lynn's travel companions. On their "avoiding Christmas 2001 trip," Paul and Lynn left the hotel room for a walk and returned to find that housekeeping had removed the bed linens along with the dog and bunny.

"I became hysterical," Lynn said. "Panicked and sobbing, I went to the front desk and poured my heart out. The desk clerk advised, with attitude, that the laundry from the resort was across the island with 10,000 pounds of other laundry from other resorts and it was unlikely that they would be able to return the items. He was basically not believing my story and giving me a 'Lady, it's only a stuffed animal' response. I was afraid that I would physically attack him. In fact, Paul had to restrain me.

"We did get the animals back, but I had to give myself a reality check. I was afraid of the woman I became and how I reacted in that moment. It wasn't healthy for me to have that strong of an emotional tie to stuffed animals. After that trip, the animals were grounded and stayed at home.

"Ruth and Leo bought me two gold angels and helped me to find the perfect picture for the locket that the angels hung from on a necklace. Once I had that necklace, it was the start and end of my day for 10 years. To not wear it almost became connected to denying Jen and Dave's existence."

In 1996, Paul suggested Lynn start jogging to release some of her anger. She could barely run two blocks without burning lungs and rubbery legs. When Lynn accomplished an entire mile, Paul convinced her to train with him to run in the Philadelphia Marathon.

Lynn ran everywhere. When you're training for a marathon, the experts say that you will eventually hit a wall and have difficulty in increasing your distance. Lynn hit the wall at 19 miles. After that point, she never attempted to go any farther. That same night, Paul asked her to marry him.

In the fall of 2006, Paul thought an animal might bring Lynn some comfort, so they went to the Humane Society. They went into each cage to interact with the cats.

"I never owned a cat," Lynn said, "so I really didn't know what to expect. I went into one particular cage and a tuxedo cat was very affectionate towards me. Paul could tell that I really liked this cat, but he reminded me that we agreed that we wouldn't get a cat until we returned home from a trip. I worried that the cat wouldn't be there when we came back in a week.

"We left the room and were headed towards the car when I asked Paul if we could go back one more time to see the cat. He agreed. When we walked into the room, the tuxedo cat knocked two cats off ledges, and on his back legs reached his paws through the bars towards me. Paul had experienced many signs from the kids over the past year and looked at me and said, 'Okay, we need to take the cat today.'

"The addition of Murray and his unconditional love in my life was huge. He has slept on my head or right up against me for the past 17 years and has been a constant comfort to me."

Some people also find comfort in visiting the cemetery. Paul and Lynn went every week for years. When they would walk up to the marker, they would never know what to expect. More often than not, it was covered with flowers, candy, cookies, cheese curls, metal confetti, angels, frogs, etc. Paul and Lynn were active contributors. In fact, all of her coat pockets had ornamental bags of confetti in them.

"Even at their gravesite, I had a routine. I would kneel down or sit on 'them' and run my fingers across their names, imagining touching their faces. My tears would leave puddles. I would pick up a piece of confetti that said 'I love you' and place it in front of each of their names. After their names, I would put another piece that said Mom. I then would tell them out loud how much I loved them.

"Jen and Dave were buried next to the most pitiful looking, Charlie Brown-type tree," Lynn said. "Ruth and Leo made it their mission to build a garden around the tree and also create a 30-foot garden along the road, all without the permission of the cemetery. They used to make me so nervous, digging dirt, planting flowers and mulching. For birthdays, Halloween and Christmas, we would decorate the tree, take balloons and roses. My dear friend, Kathy Wilson, never missed a year of going out and placing a homemade decoration on their grave. I always loved to hear that friends who never even met Jen and Dave would visit their gravesite. Slowly, over time, around the 10-year mark, I wasn't drawn to their grave, and the visits became less frequent. I no longer feel the kids' presence there. They are simply with me in my heart."

Chapter 7

Motherhood, Family, Friends

What makes a woman a mother? Is it the months she carries and nurtures her unborn child? Or does motherhood happen at the moment of birth? Perhaps a woman earns motherhood status during those 2 a.m. feedings or when she's changed her 500th diaper. Mothers watch their children board the school bus for the first time, study each report card and glow at graduations. Motherhood seems to be reaffirmed with each milestone in a child's life.

But what happens if a mother's child is violently snatched away? Is she still a mother? And how does she answer the question, "Do you have any children?"

It's a routine question, one that often follows, "Where do you live?" or "Are you married?" You might toss it at a new co-worker, the passenger in the next seat on an airplane, or when meeting someone at a social gathering.

But it's a loaded question when your only child has been murdered in a plot hatched by her husband or your son and daughter have been stabbed to death by their father. Lynn and Nancy can tell the truth about their children and relive their horror with strangers, or they can lie and leave themselves feeling they've betrayed their children by denying their existence.

Lynn used to get her hair cut in a salon in the mall, where each visit seemed to involve a new stylist. She would sit in the chair, explain what she wanted, and, like clockwork, the question would come: "Do you have any children?" Unable to deny Jennifer and David, she'd say, "Yes, two."

"How old are they and where do they go to school?" Now came the moment of truth. The truth, that they were murdered on Christmas Day 1994, would bring gasps and often tears. Lynn would find herself becoming the caretaker for a distressed stylist with scissors in her hand and tears in her eyes. After a while, it became too much of a burden. She found a regular stylist, shared her story once and avoided the dilemma.

"This was a significant issue for me almost immediately after Jen and Dave's murder," Lynn said. "Just weeks earlier, I had been just a mom looking over homework, helping Dave with his spelling words, nagging Jen to practice her clarinet, cuddling on the couch watching TV, kissing them goodnight ... just being a mom. Then, there I am ... no longer certain if I'm still a mom."

For many years, Lynn tried to avoid situations in which the question might arise. Looking busy, with a book or a computer, deters questions from strangers. It's not that the question stirs up her pain – pain is a permanent part of your life when your children have been murdered. It's the burden she's trying to avoid. "I often feel like I'm being the caretaker," she said. "I don't see the necessity of putting somebody through that pain."

Once, on a trip to an island, Lynn was relaxing with a massage when the masseuse unleashed the question. Lynn indulged in a fantasy in which Jennifer and David had grown and graduated and gone on to adulthood. She created college degrees and well-paying jobs, and the masseuse nodded in appreciation. With her deception, Lynn was able to enjoy her massage and spare the masseuse the violent details.

"If Jen and Dave were watching, they would like the jobs I chose for them," she said. She viewed that day as a win-win.

"It took many years, but I'm also fine with answering no to that question. It no longer means that I'm betraying them."

Does Nancy have children? You bet. Her child's name was Randi and she was born on December 15, 1974. "I don't say she died. I say she was murdered, because it was a violent crime," Nancy said. "I always felt that Brian Trimble stole my daughter's life. He took away the hope and excitement of being a grandmother from me," she said. "But I will always BE a mother."

And what about Lynn? Does she have kids? Of course, she does. She thinks about them every day of her life. As the years have passed, her children's friends and classmates have graduated, finished college, married and become parents. Watching her children's friends, Lynn has applauded the milestones with pain, envy and love.

In the months after her children were murdered, Lynn was embraced by their school family. "The people at North Side Elementary couldn't do enough, including the families of the children who went there," Lynn said. "They gave me David's desk and chair, and it is still proudly displayed in my home with his nametag on the front.

"David's and Jennifer's classes made me a memory box with each of their classmates' paper hands on it with their names. Their classmates overwhelmed me with beautiful notes on angels, drawings and poems. Each month, Valentine's Day, Mother's Day, etc., I received a note, a project, something from the kids letting me know how much they missed Jen and Dave and how much they cared for me and wanted me to be okay. What incredibly caring and comforting gifts they were for me!

"The principal of North Side, Ken Beard, 'adopted' me. He was a man I had known only as the principal and had met with on a few occasions to discuss David's no-so-good behavior. Ken could never talk about the loss of Jen and Dave without a tear in his eye. He thought to include me in many events at

North Side, which I always accepted, as I loved being around the kids and the teachers were so kind and supportive.

"I can remember several events early on in which the music teacher, Nancy Bonnet, organized and selected music for North Side students to sing at the state Capitol for Crime Victims' Rights Week and also at a Jen and Dave fundraising event. Again, they couldn't do enough.

"In hindsight, North Side created healing and coping opportunities for students, teachers, parents and me. Ken was an amazing man who watched over and cared for every student like they were one of his own children. His commitment to children and the education system was beyond the call of duty. Early on, I met his family, a close bond formed, and Paul and I became part of their family. I really knew I was part of the family when I was assigned dishwashing duties after a family picnic."

Then, in 2002, when Jennifer's class graduated from high school, Lynn received an invitation in the mail. The school wanted to present her with Jennifer's diploma.

At first, Lynn was appalled. "Why?" she asked, knowing the heartache that would come if she participated. Receiving that letter "was a tough day," she said.

Eventually, she and Paul decided to attend with Jen's grandparents and Shannon Wood, her best friend. Classmates, who had named a star after their pretty blond friend, referred to her as their "guiding star." They talked about feeling safe as they moved on to the next phase in their lives because they knew Jen was watching over them.

"During the entire event, I sobbed uncontrollably," Lynn said. "It was a painful milestone that I am glad that I was a part of. Afterwards, I felt a sense of peace. It was like a therapeutic purge."

As they left the graduation with Jen's diploma and a yearbook, which included a dedication to Jen, Lynn commented to Paul that the only thing missing was a tassel from a graduation cap. The words had barely left her mouth when Paul looked down and found a tassel on the ground. They remain convinced that Jennifer was with them that day.

Despite her diploma, Jennifer will always remain 10 and David, 8. Lynn has given away or stored many of their childhood things. She's learned she doesn't need items to remember Jen's smile or David's high-spiritedness. She's their mother. She always will be.

Her dear friends Ruth and Leo, who had been the children's day care providers, asked Lynn to bring boxes of childhood memories over to their house the first year. The three of them spent an entire day creating a display of each child's lifetime. Each included 100-plus items, such as baby teeth, baseball gloves, locks of hair, pictures, trophies, report cards, blankets, animals, artwork, toys and jewelry. Everything they had accomplished or loved was represented in the display.

Photos of the children taken by Leo, a professional photographer, have been hanging in Lynn's bedroom for 19 years. They are, Lynn said, "a gift that means the world to me."

Nancy, meanwhile, holds on to everything that was Randi's. She has her daughter's baby teeth, her ponytail, school papers, her wedding veil and her christening gown. She's saved her daughter's hobby horse, tricycle and toy chest. Most important to her is the journal she began writing the day Randi was born. She often turns to it, and the memories in it, to relive experiences she shared with her daughter.

Sometimes she opens the barrels containing Randi's clothes to see if she still can catch the scent of her daughter, or she listens to tapes of her daughter, just to hear that familiar voice.

All of those things make her feel good, she said, but at the same time, she knows they drain her emotionally.

Nancy and Lynn believe that everyone who has lost someone should react in his or her own way, holding on to what helps with the journey.

Those who have accompanied Nancy on her journey are invited to her celebration of life party, held annually in memory of Randi's December 15 birthday. Preparation begins a year in advance, as Nancy makes what she calls "a gift of love" for each person who attends. She also crochets blankets or knits socks for all the children, whom she calls her "little peeps." She takes off work the day before the party and prepares all the food, as she anxiously wonders who will drop by. She finds comfort in the friends who attend and their children, who sometimes ask questions about Randi.

"Brian Trimble changed how I trusted others, with his ultimate betrayal of me," Nancy said. "I have different people in my life now. I found solace with those who came to me right after Randi was killed and still remain with me. I still love everyone who has always been a part of my life, but I have respectfully placed people in groups. Tragedy changes people's lives; 10 years later, it has been a positive change for me."

Nancy and Lynn say the violent loss of a child initially is isolating. Friends and family say they understand, but they don't; they can't. While any death of a child is heart-breaking, Nancy puts the murder of a child in a separate category. "Murder is unique in its own way. There's no comparison to any other death," she said.

Sadly, they both can see why marriages and relationships fail after the loss of a child, and understand why family and friends walk away or avoid them. Simply put, individuals aren't built to carry that sort of pain for someone else. It takes a very special person to be a constant support person, particularly because mourning the loss of a child is a lifelong process.

Nancy and Lynn are fortunate to have men in their lives who are supportive almost beyond belief. They serve as partners, support systems. They mop tears and laugh with them about the good times. Lynn says a mother needs to remember those good times, as it is too easy to put those beautiful memories aside and dwell on the details of the murder.

She found great comfort after her loss in spending time with Ruth and Leo, who have been babysitting children in their home for decades.

Several weeks after the children's deaths, Ruth and Leo filled a photo album with pictures they had taken of Jen and Dave playing in the sandbox, running through the sprinkler, listening to stories and, even, sleeping. They brought it to Lynn's house. They talked about Jen, "a little mother to everybody," and David, who was mischievous, as boys can be.

Those conversations were the exception.

When your children are taken, you want to talk about them. You need to validate the fact that they existed. But Nancy and Lynn say many people think mentioning their children will make them sad or upset, as if they have somehow forgotten their grief.

Lynn also found solace in Jen's best friend, Shannon. She was 10 when Jen died, innocent enough to ask Lynn direct questions that she was more than happy to answer.

"No one would talk to me about the murder," Lynn recalled, "but Shannon, being a kid, had questions and wanted to go over every detail."

Nancy and Lynn were stuck in a Catch-22. Friends and relatives wanted them to move on, but struggled if they saw them being happy. "People have expectations," Lynn said. "If you smile, does that mean you are no longer sad? People expect to see you totally broken, and I had people in my life who wanted me to stay broken. Over time, you come to learn that that is their baggage, not yours.

"Society only gives us so much time to grieve. I'm not certain how long 'the allowable time limit' is, but fairly early on, depending on the audience … family, friends, co-workers … want us to 'move on.' In my case, they wanted the old Lynn back and sort of sent an underlying message: 'You can't change the past and really need to get over it and move on.'

"Sadly, we are forced to 'put the mask on' and pretend that we are coping and that we are doing okay. Long term, it's not okay for us to be weak, vulnerable, sobbing, lethargic or depressed. If we continue to act this way, people don't simply turn their backs, they actually run. I often think the grieving process takes longer because society is simply not as accepting as it needs to be, so we end up grieving in spurts or part time. We cover our pain with a mask. The mask goes on in public and is taken off in private. Life does go on and we have to go back to work, and we spend a lot of time in public with the mask on, with the fake feelings, and sadly we become adept at lying. Why? You quickly realize that there are not many people who truly want to hear the truth. They don't come out and say it, but we hear it loud and clear: 'Snap out of it. I can't deal with you anymore. You are bringing me down. I can only be around you in small doses.'

"The end result? People avoid, avoid, avoid.

"Family members, friends and co-workers are trying to move on themselves and, frankly, they want the old Lynn or Nancy back. Even with the people closest to you, you can't grieve full-time. You will push them away. Mostly, you grieve when you are alone. You learn to cry without making noise; you learn to cry in the shower; you tell people that you've developed allergies.

"You simply figure out ways to weave the grieving process into your everyday life. Grieving is the hardest work anyone will ever have to engage in. It's hard for the victim and also really hard for those who are in the inner circle of the victim," Lynn said.

Caught in a horrendous depression, people who are grieving cannot predict how they will feel from one day to the next. They can't commit to anything. They might agree to meet a friend for lunch, but when the day dawns, they can't muster the energy to go. "People just go away after a while," Lynn said.

Co-workers, acquaintances and neighbors often turn and look away from the women because they simply do not know what to say. "People can't deal with this. People don't know how to deal with you," Lynn said.

Others say inappropriate things. Lynn was told by some that at 34, she was young enough to have more children, as if Jen and Dave were broken china she could replace. A family member asked Lynn not to use the "m" word (murder), suggesting they refer to the loss of the children as an accident.

Others said, "Didn't you see this coming?" "Well, at least it happened when they were young; if they were older you would have been more attached to them." "I know how you feel... I lost my dog or my grandmother passed away." "When are you going to start acting like yourself again?"

These comments may be well intentioned, but they are hurtful for a grieving parent.

For years, Paul took Lynn away every Christmas to an island or a beach, somewhere that didn't look like Christmas morning in Pennsylvania. Someone once told her how lucky she was to be making those Christmas trips.

One year, on an extended family Christmas in the Florida Keys, Lynn wanted to show a video of Jen and Dave opening gifts on Christmas morning 1993. No one showed any interest. She assumed her family nixed the idea as too depressing.

Nancy's family was there immediately after Randi was murdered.

"My family came to me and stayed with me all hours of the night when Randi was killed," Nancy said. "Over time, this has changed. Some family members are still angry about the outcome, and others have simply moved on and do not want to deal with it.

"I can remember my brother-in-law Mike telling me how he simply wanted to walk up to Brian Trimble at the preliminary hearing and break his neck. Others said the same. Mike had to find an outlet to release the trauma that he had experienced from that Saturday morning (when he found out Randi was dead) through his constant involvement with the case for almost two years.

"My sister, Linda, told me that she cannot talk about it anymore. I reacted to her comments by feeling so hurt, but knew that she had to move on and focus on her new baby and son," Nancy said.

While Nancy remains close to Linda and her family, other relatives have abandoned her because of her advocacy. She's often seen on television or in newspapers and magazines talking about domestic violence and her plans to open Randi's House of Angels for children touched by abuse. Some family members don't like that, she said. They would prefer that she settle quietly back into life. They don't want her to make "a spectacle" of herself.

Some don't understand why the two women would punish themselves and keep their wounds open by emerging themselves in causes to help other crime victims. They ask, "Haven't you been through enough?"

Lynn said she tells victims only they know what they need and when, and that it's up to them to make that known. Grieving isn't a static process. What someone wants this week might not be what she needs next week.

She suggests that people ask, "What do you need?" "What can I do?" "What would you like to talk about?"

Lynn is fond of a book she read early in her journey, "When the Bough Breaks." Dr. Judith R. Bernstein writes:

> An orphan is a child without a parent. A widow or widower is a person who has lost a spouse. There is no word to identify to the outside world a parent who has lost a child. Perhaps the concept is too unthinkable. The biggest impediment is that other parents shy away from the living embodiment of their worst nightmare. If this nightmare happened to you, then it could happen to me. Besides not wanting to be reminded that such atrocities do happen, most people, even with the best of intentions, don't know what to say or do. Potential sources of support avoid the eerie and the awkward. Consequently, bereaved parents are often avoided and become victims of social ostracism.

Lynn said, "We need to become more comfortable with talking to victims. Eye contact. Two words, 'I'm sorry.' A few more words, 'I'm sorry this happened to you.' 'I can't imagine what you are going through.' 'You're in my thoughts.' 'I'll say a prayer for you.' 'I hope you're okay.' 'This must be a difficult time for you.'

"Say no more. Maybe they will talk and all you have to do is listen, or they'll thank you. A small gesture to show that you care. To this day, it is rare that someone will ask me about

Jen and Dave. Somehow, people think that it is too painful. Survivors like to be asked about their loved ones and what kind of person they were and share fond memories. Don't be afraid to mention the child's name. It won't remind parents of their loss. Trust me, they haven't forgotten. If you knew the child personally, share a memory.

"Don't be afraid to ask about details," Lynn advises. "Victims need to tell their stories over and over, especially in the early months. It's part of the process that helps them to live with the reality of their loss. It enables them to acknowledge and eventually accept their changed reality. Retelling their story is also part of remembering. Remembering and sharing both pleasant memories and painful experiences is the essence of grieving. I'm grateful that I had someone in my life willing to listen. Because the act is so incomprehensible, retelling is truly the only way that helps to make it a reality."

Nancy said that gathering thoughts and materials for this book has helped with her journey. "I see how writing this book with Lynn and retelling my story with another survivor has helped me realize that I am not alone. The feeling and changes in my life are normal. For years, I struggled with trying to remember Randi as a child. I rearranged pictures, redid the albums and could not forget the last time I saw her. Listening to Lynn tell stories about how Jen loved to draw pictures and Dave's love for baseball helped me remember Randi as a child."

From the beginning, it falls on those most deeply wounded to tell the rest of us how we should act.

"I learned very quickly how uncomfortable Jen and Dave's murder made other people, even my family," Lynn said. "The pain and the loss were mine, but in almost every encounter, I found the first move was mine, as well. Rarely would any-one speak of 'it.' I needed to speak first and to let others know that they can talk about 'it' with me. I didn't do that, but in hindsight, I needed to be the one to tell people who knew Jen and Dave that I still wanted to talk about them and they could talk about them, too. If I wanted certain people to come by, I needed to invite them.

"For the most part, my family dealt with their deaths by clamming up. Or, they thought by talking about Jen and Dave they would hurt me further, and no one in my family wanted me to endure any more pain or sadness. I should have told them that I needed to talk; I needed them to listen. I needed for them to talk about their feelings and also talk about Jen and Dave. I needed to hear about all of their wonderful memories."

After the horror of that Christmas morning, Lynn battled to hold herself together. She survived moment by moment. It was grossly unfair that it fell to her to coach other people.

"But there it is," she said. "For every friend and relative who could move to my side gracefully, there were two or more who would rather avoid me or reach out to me only if I reached out first.

"My circle of support, in essence my new family, in the first few years was extremely small. It included my psychologist, Paul, two co-workers, three friends, and my parents. I couldn't even begin to count the number of people over the years who have avoided me."

When Paul initially took Lynn to see Jeff Verrecchio, who would become her therapist, the psychologist saw a woman in deep shock. He said Lynn looked to him like someone who had survived a horrendous car accident. She had "a deer in the headlights" look.

At first, he said, she kept going by talking and taking medicine for anxiety. Lynn had Paul. Not everyone has a Paul in her life, but Jeff said everyone needs a sounding board, someone who is nonjudgmental and who will listen.

Lynn eventually began talking to Jeff. For an entire year, he said, they talked of nothing but the murders of Jen and Dave. "There were no other conversations that happened," he said.

Eventually, he discovered a woman of great "spirit, character and drive. It was in honor of her children and their spirit that she went on to do great things," he said.

Jeff said our society doesn't know how to deal with victims because we have been taught to avoid emotions. While children learn the ABCs, no one teaches them how to deal with what they are feeling.

"Our greatest emotional culprit is our culture that doesn't educate us about emotions," he said.

If a victim doesn't find an outlet, the person can become fixed on the trauma and unable to move on. Families and friends, he said, must be willing to listen nonjudgmentally. If the victim wants to talk, let her, he advised. And if she wants to hear their thoughts and memories, they should share them.

Lynn still recalls an email her sister, Nancy, sent her on April 16, 2000, a day that should have been David's 14th birthday and two days past Jen's 16th. It said, "Lynn, I wish I could do more for you than just hug you when you need it. Jen and Dave have been on my mind all week. Please remember, Lynn, although we don't get to talk much, you are always on my mind and in my heart. I love you very much."

Lynn said she read the email a hundred times or more and each time found it comforting.

A simple thought. "I'm thinking of you." A simple remembrance. "Your children have been on my mind." And, yet, we make it so difficult.

The Mention of Their Names

The mention of my children's names
May bring tears to my eyes,
But it never fails to bring
music to my ears.
If you are really my friend,
Let me hear the beautiful music of their names
it soothes my broken heart
And sings to my soul.

--- *Author Unknown.*

Chapter 8

Religion

From the beginning of time, people have pondered the role of God. Whatever they have called Him, whatever form He has taken, for most He seems to be an all-knowing spirit. While many seek solace in the belief that something better awaits after this world, people for generations have debated just what role God plays in our earthly lives. Is He an observer or a puppet master? Does He watch while we stumble through life trying to find answers, or does He move us from situation to situation like pieces on a chessboard?

Those who grow up with the Bible quickly learn stories of God's anger and revenge. Only the chosen ones on the ark escaped the great flood. For her disobedience, Lot's wife was transformed into a pillar of salt. Job, although he was a righteous man, suffered the loss of his money, children and health.

So it is only natural for a mother to ask God why He allowed her child to suffer a horrible fate. A mother will wonder what she did wrong to be punished so cruelly.

"I was definitely angry with God," Lynn said. "Why would God ever allow or cause this to happen? Two precious children, whose deaths have affected so many people. In the beginning, my world and beliefs were shattered. I doubted God and His existence."

Nancy had a similar reaction. She had followed her upbringing, raised her daughter in the Catholic Church and sent her to Catholic school. In her mind, she had done everything right. So when Randi's life ended so horribly, Nancy found herself wondering why God was punishing her.

"I was angry with God," Nancy said. "Why did He let this happen to Randi, to me?"

Nancy blamed herself. She inventoried her life. Surely she had done something so terrible that God had allowed this punishment.

Randi had been her world. "She gave meaning to my life and made me feel complete," Nancy said. "I have the rest of my life and I don't have her."

Answers to such questions aren't always forthcoming. And just as every doctor/patient relationship doesn't always click, finding the right spiritual adviser sometimes requires testing the waters. The priest or minister or rabbi who was so helpful to an acquaintance might not be the right fit for another person.

Lynn recalls that soon after her children were murdered a member of the clergy told her the children's deaths were God's will. "I looked at him as though he was nuts. God's will? I do not think that God picked Jen and Dave and said, 'Their father will stab them 10 times and then take his own life.'"

He obviously wasn't going to be her source of comfort.

Nancy found some relief through talking with Father Chester P. Snyder, a Catholic priest retired from a parish in Mechanicsburg, Pa. "God didn't take your daughter," he told her. "God's way is not to treat us like pieces on a chessboard, but to walk with us."

Father Snyder reminded Nancy that we aren't in heaven yet. Instead, we live in an imperfect world where bad things happen.

When Nancy told Father Snyder that she will never have peace until she is dead and reunited with Randi, Father Snyder told her to hold on to her expectations. After all, he asked, "Shouldn't heaven be more than what we have here on earth?"

Nancy grabbed at that statement, so simple, yet profound. She talks often of being reunited with Randi after death. Why wouldn't that be her idea of heaven?

While Father Snyder offered comfort to Nancy, not every clergyman hits the right note. Lynn has learned through her work with victims that some clergy, just like some laypeople, hide behind stock phrases because they have no idea what to say.

"Telling someone whose child was murdered that there was some hidden purpose behind the tragedy or you need to continue to trust in Him, as someday we will understand His plan, does not bring comfort," Lynn said. Neither do reassurances that time heals, the dead are in a better place, or God never gives us more than we can handle. "These type of statements conflict with what the parent is feeling, which is devastation and hopelessness. When the death is recent, victims often struggle with these types of comments, as they cannot allow God and the violent act of murder to co-exist.

"Bringing God into the discussion and connecting Him in some way to the act can be unsettling. The victim's first thoughts are, 'Why would God ever allow this to happen?' The parent needs to have their anguish acknowledged and accepted," Lynn said.

Lynn's path toward peace was long and winding. She was, for the most part, led along the path by the Rev. Patrick Wirick Jr. of Epiphany Lutheran Church in suburban Harrisburg. Pastor Pat was drawn to Lynn by members of his congregation, which included one of the detectives investigating Jen and Dave's murders. Police had noticed ritualistic aspects to their deaths. Among them were the words Tom had written on his body, "King of kings, Lord of lords." Investigators also found numerous documents on Tom's computer. His words offer a look into a deteriorating mind:

"ANYONE WANT A LESSON ON THE BIBLE NAMELY THE BOOK OF REVELATIONS? I'LL GIVE IT TO YOU ANYWAYS.

CHAPTER 1 – DEALS WITH CHRIST EXPLAINING TO JOHN WHAT'S IN STORE FOR US. NOW REMEMBER IT'S CHRIST EXPLAINING TO JOHN WHAT'S GOING TO HAPPEN SO DON'T FORGET THAT.

VERSE 20 – DEALS WITH THE SEVEN STARS AND SEVEN CANDLESTICKS. IF YOU LOOK ON BLUE MOUNTAIN IN HARRISBURG THERE IS A TOWER WTH THREE LIGHTS ON THE MAST AND FOUR LIGHTS AT THE BASE. THESE LIGHTS REPRESENT THE SEVEN STARS. THE SEVEN CANDLESTICKS ARE SEVEN LIGHTS ON THE OUTSIDE OF SOMEONE'S HOME (MINE).

CHAPTERS 2 & 3 GIVE A DESCRIPTION OF SOMEONE WHO'S DEAF IN THEIR LEFT EAR. THAT'S WHY YOU HAVE "HE THAT HAS AN EAR" THAT STATEMENT REPRESENTS ONE WHO HAS ONE GOOD EAR (ME)

THIS POOR JERK WALKS WITHIN THE SEVEN CANDLESTICKS AND WHEN HE LOOKS OUT HIS FRONT WINDOW GUESS WHAT HE SEES. THAT'S RIGHT HE SEE SEVEN STARS TO HIS RIGHT.

VERSE 9 - THIS POOR JERK IS TO HAVE A HARD LIFE AND BE POOR BUT HE'S ALSO RICH IN OTHER THINGS (ANYONE WANT TO GUESS WHAT HE'S RICH IN)

VERSE 14 – IDOL WORSHIP LIKE THE HARE KRISHNA DUDES (I HAVE $300 WORTH OF THEIR BOOKS AND HAVE PRACTICED THEIR CRAP ALSO IN MY DAYS IN BETWEEN WIVES. I WAS QUITE A FORNICATOR WHICH I'M NOT PROUD ABOUT. I'VE BEEN MARRIED TWICE AND DIVORCED TWICE WITH TWO CHILDREN FROM EACH WIFE. I HAVE QUITE A LIFE HISTORY DON'T YOU THINK)

CHAPTER 19 VERSE 12 – THERE ARE KEY DESCRIPTIVE STATEMENTS IN CHAPTERS 2 AND 3 THAT SHOW UP IN THE LATER CHAPTERS. SEE CHAPTER 12 FOR A DESCRIPTION OF MY MOTHER.

MY RELATIVES TOLD ME I ALMOST DIED AT BIRTH. ALSO I WAS BORN IN SPARROWS POINT, MARYLAND IN MY GRANDMOTHERS HOUSE. THIS HOUSE WAS ON THE PROPERTY OF A STEEL COMPANY. GUESS WHAT THE NAME OF THE STEEL COMPANY IS. MY BIRTHDAY IS 7-15-48 WHICH IS THE BEGINNING OF THE SUMMER HARVEST AND A RELIGIOUS TIME IN THE OLD TESTAMENT. 1948 IS ALSO THE YEAR ISRAEL BECAME A NATION.

VERSE 20 – DESCRIPTION OF MY SECOND WIFE, TRUST ME THE WOMAN IS AN OUTRIGHT WITCH.

VERSE 23 – GOD WILL KILL HER CHILDREN WITH DEATH AND ALL THE CHURCHES (HE THAT WALKS WITHIN THE 7 CANDLESTICKS) SHALL KNOW I AM HE THAT SEARCHETH THE REINS AND HEARTS. HE'S GOING TO KILL MY CHILDREN (DAVID AND JENNIFER) SEE THE OLD TESTAMENT FOR KING DAVID AND THE LOSS OF HE'S FIRST BORN CHILD. IT'S NOT AS BAD AS YOU THINK BECAUSE CHILDREN ENTER HEAVEN AND ARE WITH GOD.

MY FAVORITE CHAPTERS ARE 12, 19 & 21. CHAPTER 19 VERSES 7, 8 & 9 GIVE A DESCRIPTION OF THE LAMB'S BRIDE TO BE (THIS IS NOT CHRIST LIKE EVERYONE THINKS OR NEW JERUSALEM OR ISRAEL). CHAPTER 19 IS ABOUT HE THAT OVERCOMES AND HAS A NAME NO ONE KNOWS AND HE SHALL RULE THE NATIONS WITH A ROD OF IRON). MY BIRTHDAY OF 7-15-48 IS A DESCRIPTION OF ME BY VERSES. SEE VERSES 7, 12 & 15. YOU GET THE 12 BY ADDING THE TWO NUMBERS IN MY YEAR FOR THOSE OF YOU THAT AREN'T TO SMART.

SWITCHING GEARS FOR A MINUTE. DID YOU GUYS AT WROZ 101.3 KNOW YOUR IN THE BIBLE! I'M SO SICK OF LISTENING TO THE BULLSHIT YOU HAVE BEEN FEEDING ME THE LAST TWO MONTHS. THIS CRAP WITH YOUR CO-WORKER HAS LONG SINCE WORN OUT. SORRY D.F. BUT SOMEONE ELSE WAS

PERSONNALY PICKED OUT BY A HIGHER AUTHORITY. THE FEW TIMES I TRIED TO DUMP HER I PAID DEARLY FOR IT (GOD HAS CONTROL OVER MY MIND, SENSES AND BODILY FUNCTIONS. WHEN THE TIME COMES I'LL EXPLAIN TO HER WHY I DID THOSE THINGS AND NOT YOU GUYS. BUT IF ANY OF YOU GET THE CHANGE, TELL HER I REALLY DO LOVE HER!!!!! BY THE WAY HOW DID YOU GET THE OTHER FM'S IN ON THIS. CAN THESE GUYS TUNE INTO ME? I WAS IN THE SUPERMARKET THE OTHER DAY AND I THOUGHT TO MYSELF THIS CHECK-OUT GIRL IS CUTE. NEXT THING SHE'S LOOKING RIGHT AT ME WITH THIS BIG SMILE. ARE MY THOUGHTS OPEN TO EVERYONE?

I KNOW WHAT IT'S LIKE TO HAVE FIRE IN MY EYES. BOY DID GOD GIVE ME A BAD TEMPER AND NOTHING I DO SEEMS TO CONTROL IT. JUST ASK SEVEN TEACHERS AT LOWER PAXTON JR HIGH SCHOOL WHO'S BUTT I KICKED IN FRONT OF 1200 KIDS IN THE GYM. THERE'S OTHER EXAMPLES BUT THAT ONE IS A BIG ONE (I WAS 14 YEARS OLD SAME AGE AS KING DAVID WHEN HE TOOK ON THE 6'9" GIANT AND KILLED HIM WITH A STONE)

The writings go on and on.

The detective approached Pastor Pat looking for answers and shared the documents from Tom's computer and the handwritten list he had left on his end table: Cancel the life insurance, join a church, have Jennifer and David baptized and "kill Jen and Dave."

Although the baptisms never took place, Tom proceeded with his horrific ending. As Pastor Pat looked at the documents Tom had left, at the words he had written on his body, and events on the night of the children's deaths, he felt that Tom had scripted a scene from the Apocalypse. "In his mind," Pastor Pat said, "I think he was giving Jen and Dave the best Christmas present possible: Jesus and Heaven, while at the same time taking them away from everyone he thought was trying to keep him away from his children."

Although he hadn't met Lynn at the time of the murders, Pastor Pat knew Tom and the children. For part of his life, Tom had followed the precepts of Hare Krishna, which became popular in the United States in the late 1960s and 1970s and follows core beliefs based on traditional Hindu scriptures dating back thousands of years. But in the last eight months of his life, he became heavily involved in his own brand of Christianity.

Being asked to make sense of Tom's twisted religious logic and the senseless crime that ensued was a gargantuan task, even for a man of God.

Jen and Dave sometimes attended Sunday school and church with friends from Pastor Pat's congregation. He remembers Jen as a friendly, quiet, shy girl who fit in naturally and played and giggled with the other girls. David was energetic and playful.

"The church was a wonderful place for small boys," Pastor Pat said. "Lots of rooms and places to explore, places to hide and lots of diversions on the way to Sunday school and church. There were many conversations that began something like, 'Guys, we go around the table, not over the table, to get to our seat,' or 'Stop hiding under the table; it's time to go to class now.'"

Sometimes Tom brought Jen and Dave to Pastor Pat's Lutheran church, but the pastor didn't know their father well. Tom occasionally would ask about having Jen and Dave baptized, but he never followed up or made an appointment to talk about it, perhaps because Pastor Pat had told him he would not baptize the children without the consent of their mother.

Pastor Pat recalled that Tom sometimes expressed religious ideas that were rather extreme and that he clearly did not like being challenged. Tom stopped attending the church shortly after he was confronted about visiting patients at a local hospital, where he presented himself as being a part of Epiphany's pastoral ministry. He wasn't. His bizarre behavior at the hospital had frightened some patients and prompted a call to Pastor Pat, who made it clear to Tom that his actions were unacceptable. Despite several efforts on his part, Pastor Pat never saw or heard from Tom again.

"I did not think Tom was of a sound mind," Pastor Pat said, "but neither did I think he was a threat or danger to anyone."

When Pastor Pat returned from visiting family out of town for Christmas 1994, he found several disturbing messages on his answering machine. His first thought was for members of his church who were close to Lynn and her children.

"There were two things happening here," he said. "The first was dealing with the brutal death of two children for whom there was a great deal of care and love. The second was the need to be a source of comfort and support to Lynn."

Initially, he shared with members of his congregation his faith and his understanding of God.

"This is what I believe," he said. "This was not God's will. This did not happen because Lynn or Jen or Dave did something wrong. This did not happen because there are not enough little angels in heaven or it was their 'time' or any of the other things people might say because they don't know what to say and feel the need to say something, and somewhere along the line they got the idea these words were comforting.

"The second major concern I had was for classmates and friends of Jen and Dave who could not be shielded from the horror of what had happened to them," he said. "One of my biggest concerns was that some children might think their parents might kill them like Jen and Dave's father had killed them. I tried to show our kids different ways they could see their parents could be trusted, even if they might yell or punish sometimes. I also tried to help parents see that some of the things they might say or do could be terribly misinterpreted and to make an extra special effort to show how much they cared for their children."

Lynn had not been affiliated with a church prior to the children's deaths. A friend invited her to attend a memorial Mass for Jen and Dave at a local Catholic church. To this day, Lynn remains dumbstruck with the words of the priest, who told those assembled, "God has chosen two roses amongst all of us thorns. He has taken these children from us for he is angry with us because we are not doing the work He asks of us."

Then, in a final blow in a separate conversation, he told Lynn that Jen and Dave had not gone to heaven because they had not been baptized. Lynn reeled at the thought that her children were not in heaven. In the weeks and months that followed, she contemplated suicide. Without her children, her life seemed to have no purpose.

Meanwhile, Pastor Pat asked mutual friends how Lynn was coping. When they said not well, he reached out to her. The first time they talked, it was apparent that Lynn was deciding whether or not to fight for her life. But they continued to meet and talk. Lynn wanted to know if her children were all right, if they could forgive her for not protecting them, if they knew how much she missed them and if they were in heaven.

"The scripture tells us God is love," Pastor Pat told her. "We love because God first loved us, and where there is love, there is God. Faith assures us there is nowhere else they can be than living in the presence of a loving Father."

Lynn was drawn to join Epiphany because her children and close friends went there and by her ability to confide in Pastor Pat. His intent, she said, was never to "fix her," but to listen, comfort and support.

One day Lynn posed a question, and Pastor Pat thought his answer might drive her away. "Lynn asked me if I thought Tom was in hell for what he had done," Pastor Pat said. "We were standing at the top of the steps going to the parking lot of the church. I honestly feared this might be the last time I talked with Lynn because I had no way of knowing how she would hear my answer. I do not think Tom is in hell. I think what he did is a sure sign of a sick and broken soul. God takes what is sick and heals it. God takes what is broken and makes it whole. I believe this to be as true for Tom as it is for everyone. In one sense, the person who killed Jen and Dave and took his own life does not exist anymore."

Despite the answer, which caused Lynn pain, confusion and unsettledness, Lynn did return. She might not have liked his answer at the time, but she valued Pastor Pat's honesty.

A few years later, she turned to Pastor Pat with an important life question. Paul Shiner wanted to marry her. Lynn was uncertain. She loved Paul with all her heart, but she feared that committing to him would somehow be a rejection of her children. She wondered if she had a right to be happy.

Pastor Pat told Lynn that the love for a mate is not born of the same place as the love we have for our children. It fills a different part of our soul. He assured her that she, who had lost so much already, would take nothing from Jen and Dave if she married Paul. "Please don't give up the most precious thing you have left," he begged her. From the moment Pastor Pat had met Paul, he had no doubt that Lynn found in him the one she could trust and the one she wanted to trust. She had told Pastor Pat on several occasions she feared what her life would have been without Paul.

Pastor Pat married Lynn and Paul along the Susquehanna River on a sunny day with blue skies, a few clouds and a bit of a breeze. Both are now committed to supporting the mission of Epiphany Lutheran Church, where Lynn serves on the church council, and both spend countless hours every spring helping make chocolate eggs that the church sells to raise funds and to create an opportunity for fellowship.

Similar doubts about the right to be happy have plagued Nancy. Like Lynn, she has found herself frozen and questioning how she can be happy when Randi is dead.

Nancy recalls going out with friends to a club one night after Randi's death. She and Greg Green were dancing when she looked up and saw the district attorney who had prosecuted her daughter's killers. She was embarrassed, ashamed actually, that she was enjoying herself.

Nancy, whose grandparents had emigrated from Mexico, was raised in a culture that dictated a strong belief in Catholicism. But as she grew into adulthood, she sometimes found herself at odds with church teachings, especially those held by some older priests.

Nancy graduated from high school in 1973 and ran off to marry Randi's father the following January. When her dream shattered because of abuse and isolation, her shame, her faith and her upbringing prevented her from seeking help.

Because Nancy had not married in a Catholic ceremony, she was reluctant to turn to the church. She feared the priests would question the validity of her marriage and her right to come to them. But even though she has not been a regular in the church pews, Nancy still professes her religion. "I am a Catholic and I will always be," she said.

So it was natural for her to turn to Father Snyder for comfort and understanding. He helped her understand that guilt comes not from others but is a judgment she makes on herself.

"I will always feel responsible for not seeing signs or acting upon uncertainties," Nancy said, "but I alone deal with that."

Father Snyder came into Randi's life when she was a student at Bloomsburg University and he was the college chaplain. When she and Brian decided to marry, she asked Father Snyder to perform the ceremony. Sadly, less than three years later, he assisted with her funeral.

Nancy went to Father Snyder after Brian's arrest, trying to make sense of the crime and her emotional devastation.

He told her then something that sounds now like a prediction come true: Her future would be different, and that future would test her morality. He insists that the drive within Nancy, the goodness and determination to make her life count for something, was always there. Randi's death didn't change her, he said. Rather, it brought out qualities that had been there and channeled them in a new direction. Nancy walked away holding onto a phrase: Whatever we do in our lives we should always question what fruit it bears unto others.

After the murder, Nancy had asked Father Snyder about the death penalty. The district attorney had asked Nancy her feelings, but at the time, with her world shattered, Nancy couldn't formulate a response. She had grown up with the Ten

Commandments. She believed in "Thou shalt not kill." Now the law was asking her if the men who killed her daughter should be put to death.

"I had to go to the priest," she said. "I needed religion to help guide me and to have someone tell me I wasn't committing a sin if I wanted the death penalty."

Father Snyder said that the Catholic Church teaches that the death penalty is seldom right. If an evil person remains a threat to society, then perhaps the death penalty might be the only solution. But those circumstances are extremely rare. The death penalty, he said, is simply a way of seeking revenge. It's not a cure, because the victim's family is still left with loss and pain.

In Nancy's case, it never came to that. Both Brian Trimble and Blaine Norris pleaded guilty to their crimes in order to avoid the possibility of the death penalty. That they are being punished is little consolation to a mother who has lost her daughter.

"Today I feel very strongly that I should have had an active role" in deciding their fate, Nancy said. "I know this sounds terrible, but I wanted to go to trial for Blaine Norris. I wanted him dead. He's the one who killed Randi."

Despite her search for answers, Nancy is not at peace. She still wrestles with the question of what she might have done to deserve what the fates, or God, heaped upon her.

"For years I have suffered from guilt placed upon me from family members," she said. "My family values are very strong and demanding. That will never go away. Understanding how and what I could have done to prevent Randi's murder never leaves me. My life was protecting Randi.

"Father Snyder's guidance helped me to see that feeling guilty and holding myself responsible is not uncommon. He gave me hope that over time I will learn to manage and deal with the guilt."

Meanwhile, several years into her journey, Lynn was asked to share her story as well as her perspective on grief and loss with a group of 150 seminarians at Saint Charles Borromeo

Seminary in suburban Philadelphia. One of the questions was, "What should clergy say to a victim who is grieving and in distress?"

She told them not to be afraid to make eye contact. Victims crave simple words, such as "I'm sorry."

"Depending on the relationship you have with the family, pray for them or with them," she said. The prayers should be simple and ask for strength and comfort for the grieving. They should ask that those grieving be surrounded with love, care and support in the days ahead. Blessing or honoring the person who is deceased, asking in prayer that he or she may live forever in our memories, also is comforting. Pray that we not lose the blessing of the love we have been given to the grief that comes from the loss we suffer. Pray for the strength and help to get through today. It is vital to know that this is just one of many prayers – let the prayers speak to the moment. Let tomorrow's prayer speak for tomorrow."

If clergy choose to send a prayer or sympathy card to the grieving, Lynn suggests that it should be simple and offer hope, such as "May God bless you and be with you, even when the darkness is overwhelming. Know that we love you and are praying with you during this difficult time." Pastor Pat added, "The scriptures are full of images that can speak beautifully and honestly to the moment."

Among those he mentioned were the Psalmist's "Out of the depths I cry to you…," Paul's "I am certain that neither life nor death … can separate us from the love of God," and Jesus' "I am with you always…"

Let victims lead the way. If they want to talk, they will.

"The greatest comfort," Lynn said, "comes from listening without judgment and creating an atmosphere that gives permission for the person whose loved one was murdered to feel whatever they feel at the moment. Allowing someone to express even the most outrageous feelings without judgment is the vital gift of acceptance. If clergy try to impose order or reason, it most likely will fall on deaf ears. An accepting presence is the greatest gift possible.

"Honest comments, such as, 'I can't imagine what it must be like for you,' signal that you are receptive to hear what it's like and you are opening the door for communication," Lynn said. "Silence, accompanied by a comforting gesture and a posture that indicates you are listening, is helpful. When a tragic event occurs and a grief-stricken parent asks why, he or she really doesn't expect a theological dissertation. There is no answer. There is no right thing to say. The only reasonable response is to reiterate what the parent is feeling, that the death is unfair, the death is wrong, the death was a hideous tragedy."

The advice Lynn offered the seminarians can be extended to anyone faced with a person who has suffered a tragedy, Pastor Pat said. Don't promise things will get better with time or someday this will make sense. "I know that I find no comfort from such things, and I do not think they are representative of the God Jesus calls Father," he said. "There is much in the world that is not the way God wants it to be. Yet God comes to our pain, turmoil and suffering and surrounds us with love, care, concern, help, hope, trust, promise of friends, family, acquaintances and even total strangers to get us through the days we could not get through by ourselves.

"Forget about needing to be strong for someone, just be there for the person. Tears are not a sign of weakness; there can be much healing in tears. Do not judge people for the way they grieve – different people grieve in different ways. Know that none of us gets through life without scars on our souls. They remind us of what we have been through and of those who were there with us," Pastor Pat said.

Lynn offers one more important piece of advice for clergy and others: Don't be afraid to mention the child's name. Share your memories and encourage others to share memories of the child, such as the time they did something kind or played a sport or displayed a particular attribute. "It won't remind parents of their loss," Lynn said. "Trust me, they haven't forgotten. Also, acknowledge the 'tougher days,' such as birthdays, the anniversary of the death, holidays. A simple note, text, email, call or hand on the shoulder speaks volumes. To a victim, it says you care, you haven't forgotten and you hope that they are okay."

If Lynn once shook her fist at God, she has moved beyond that now.

"In the beginning, I doubted God and his existence. Over time, through listening to my pastor's sermons, our talks and much reading, I knew that God was not to blame.

"I believe that God has chosen to empower each of us with the ability to make choices. As long as God gives us this ability, there will always be those who will suffer at the hands of those who make bad choices. I no longer question God. He has his reasons, and someday I will understand why. Yes, I am at peace with God."

Chapter 9

Media

The murders of blond-haired Jennifer and David Snead, killed by their father early on Christmas morning while they slept in his comfortable suburban home, set off a media frenzy. The nightmare scene deeply affected police and emergency workers called to the home that Christmas morning. It left a stunned community in disbelief. How, everyone asked, could a father kill two innocent children expecting to awaken to Santa's bounty?

The murder of Nancy Chavez's daughter, Randi, brought a similar reaction, with an added ingredient of fear. Randi was a bright, attractive, college-educated woman murdered in the early evening in her own garage in a suburban community. People in the vicinity wondered if a madman was on the loose. If a stranger had done this to Randi, were they and their families in danger, too?

"People are scared," a neighbor told a Patriot-News reporter a few days after Randi's murder. "The person who did this is still out there."

The deaths of Jennifer and David, and later of Randi, left them labeled forever as crime victims. But the crimes also created living victims: Lynn, Nancy and everyone who loved their children. The media, in their efforts to understand and explain the deaths of this trio of unlikely victims, focused on the grieving mothers, bringing a barrage of unwelcome and unwanted attention.

Had they been famous people, such as politicians, CEOs, or entertainers, they could have called forth an entourage of media handlers. Their spokesmen or spokeswomen would have set the rules, reined in the herds of curious reporters, and issued statements on their clients' behalf.

But no such barrier separates people such as Lynn and Nancy from the prying media, whose questions and prodding can leave a victim feeling bruised and battered.

Lynn recalls a family member turning on the television news in the days following her children's deaths. "I heard for the first time on TV that my son was awake at the time of his murder and had defense wounds on his hands as his father stabbed him over and over. This image is forever etched in my mind as I think of what must have been going through my son's head as his own father stabbed him.

"If it was possible, I sobbed harder," she said. "Why wouldn't someone tell me and my family first? To this day, I question how that piece of news served the public good, or was it reported to add shock value to the story?"

Reporters dogged friends and acquaintances of Lynn's. They asked if she had a drinking problem. Did she do drugs? Had she had an affair while married to the children's father? Perhaps they expected to find some fault in Lynn that could explain Tom Snead's final actions. Perhaps the answer lay in some dark secret corner of Lynn's life. If she had vices, reporters could reassure the public that such horrors happen only to people who bring them on themselves. To Lynn, it seemed as if they were trying to blame her for the deaths of her children.

If learning about her son's final moments on television wasn't bad enough, her dismay was compounded during her children's funeral. Reporters camped outside the funeral home, hounding friends as they arrived to pay their respects.

One even came into the funeral home uninvited and had to be asked to leave. Eventually, the funeral director ordered the media to leave the property. They moved across the street and focused their zoom lenses on those exiting the funeral home.

Lynn had chosen to bury Jennifer and David in one coffin. To comfort them, and herself, she had placed several meaningful items in the casket. At the cemetery, camera operators were kept about a football field away behind a row of trees. When it was time to whisper her final good-byes, she kneeled down under the tent set aside for family and placed two roses atop their casket.

Her final words and the cherished items placed in the casket became fodder for the media. The following day, the front page of the newspaper carried a story that began with the words: "A Cabbage Patch doll guarded Jennifer. A truck was parked by her brother David. Toys and photographs of loved ones were tucked between the two children, who were laid to rest in the same casket, together, still."

Two break-out quotes near a photograph of the casket featured words the pastor used during the service and Lynn's final words to her children. To this day, Lynn wonders how reporters had heard what she had whispered, because even those sitting nearby didn't hear.

"This felt so wrong," she said. "I felt so violated. What right does a total stranger have to enter into a place that is for those who loved my children, just for the insensitive desire to put a few bells and whistles on their news article by detailing such private final moments? How dare they share my final whispered words and invade such a private, devastating time in my life and post it on the front page of the paper? How does revealing personal, intimate details prevent further crime and protect the community?"

Although Nancy has saved all the newspapers from the time of Randi's murder, she has never read a word. "I'm afraid to read the details of it," she said.

Nancy's disenchantment with the media came at a national level. After Randi's death, she had been contacted by

"Dateline," which wanted to detail the bizarre story of Blaine Norris, Brian Trimble and the horror movie that clenched their friendship and became an excuse for Randi's murder. Nancy agreed to cooperate, with stipulations. Among them was her insistence that there be no crime scene photos. The writer, she said, "played on me." She told Nancy she, too, was a victim of domestic violence and understood how she felt.

When the show aired in January 2006, Nancy was devastated to see photos of her beloved Randi on the floor of her garage in a pool of blood. She felt as if Randi was being victimized again. She was horrified to hear Brian's co-workers, people who didn't know Randi, say her daughter refused to give him lunch money, as if that somehow justified his actions.

In her anger, she turned to her victim advocate and someone from the Pennsylvania Coalition Against Domestic Violence. They traveled to New York to meet with Dateline's executive producer, who listened politely. But, Nancy said, "He didn't hear anything that I said." Nancy asked for more sensitivity for the families of victims and suggested the show offer the phone numbers of domestic violence hotlines. He refused, and said, "This is what people want."

The trip, she said, confirmed her thoughts that "crime is a commodity for the media."

Despite what happened with "Dateline," Nancy placed her trust in two young men who wanted to make a documentary they called "Rough Cut." It outlines the story of Blaine Norris' plan to make a horror movie about a group of five hikers murdered on the Appalachian Trail by the ghost of a coal-mining baron. The movie, which was to be called "Through Hike," was tied to Randi's murder because Blaine needed money, and Brian's ability to benefit financially from Randi's death provided a partial motive.

Woven throughout "Rough Cut" are interviews with the actors and police detectives and photos of Randi and Brian's wedding. Brian, who worked with Blaine at Capital Blue Cross, told Randi that he wanted to invest $5,000 in the production, which Blaine envisioned as the next "Blair Witch Project."

Randi, working two jobs to prepare for a day when her husband would be disabled by multiple sclerosis, quashed that idea.

Brian was to be the cinematographer, according to the actors. He took their headshots for a website about the movie. But Blaine said Brian would be unable to take on the task of shooting the movie because his multiple sclerosis prevented him from walking the rough trail. Instead, he agreed to loan Blaine his expensive photography equipment. Randi quashed that idea as well, persuading her husband that it would be foolish to lend thousands of dollars of equipment to strangers.

Undeterred, Blaine used his credit card to buy his own equipment and fell deeply in debt as he financed "Through Hike."

Actors recalled that Blaine was nerdy, methodical and well-organized. They described him as fascinated with the game "Dungeons and Dragons." He would shoot scenes all day and edit film all night, seldom pausing to sleep. His passion for the movie was so intense that his wife, Wendy, left him, taking their young son.

In "Rough Cut," actors and friends of Blaine's called him odd. They said he had multiple affairs and belonged to swingers clubs. He lined one wall of his apartment with a collection of medieval weapons.

"Blaine had a real liking for doing things that you weren't supposed to do," one friend said.

"Rough Cut" opens with Brian's 911 call at 8:29 p.m. on Jan. 10, 2003. It flashes repeatedly to scenes from Brian and Randi's wedding. The couple dance, pose for pictures, repeat vows, and eat wedding cake. These scenes morph to others, of Randi's garage, where her body was found, and her house, ransacked, supposedly by a burglar-turned-killer.

Nancy appears in "Rough Cut." You see her in scenes from her daughter's wedding. You hear the disbelief that hangs in her voice as she says of Brian, "My daughter loved him till the minute she died."

Nancy says the documentary makers always treated her with respect, so she agreed to attend the premiere of the movie at a local theater. But the evening devastated her. "I had never heard the 911 call and could not get Brian's voice out of my head and how he was pleading for someone to help his wife." She forced herself to smile, but she was aching inside at the brutal truth on the big screen.

Despite her disillusionment with the media, Nancy admits to being an avid viewer of true crime television, including "Dateline" and "48 Hours." "I'm compelled to watch murders and real people," she said. "I also think I do it because I don't want to feel like I'm all alone."

Both Lynn and Nancy have given voice to their experiences. Lynn has delved into the truths of a newsroom. "Something I find ironic," she said, "is the fact that if you are a journalist and your assignment is that of a financial nature, you would have had significant training to grasp the economy. You would have learned about stock trends, bear and bull markets, the workings of the Dow and the S&P, what triggers rising interest rates and more.

"The same goes for a sportswriter. Can you imagine a sportswriter who doesn't know the basic rules of football, baseball or basketball? It wouldn't happen," she said.

Crime reporters, however, are often the youngest, most inexperienced reporters in the room. Often, theirs is an entry-level job that requires eager young reporters to work nights, holidays and weekends. They quickly learn the workings of the criminal justice system, and they may develop excellent contacts at the surrounding police departments.

"But," Lynn asks, "What type of training do crime reporters receive on victimization issues prior to their first assignment? Do they understand trauma? In domestic violence cases, do they know why abusers continue to abuse? Do reporters know that every county has victim service agencies that employ advocates who will explain the services available, the workings of the juvenile and adult justice systems, and the rights to which all victims are entitled?"

In her efforts to open the eyes of those writing the news, Lynn met with newspaper reporters in a seminar in Harrisburg. "I asked the reporters in the room to put themselves in my shoes and read to them a story I prepared on the first 72 hours after the death of my children to let them know about the physical and emotional impact of losing a loved one as well as the impact their actions and words had on my life."

Two days later, an editor from the newspaper in Harrisburg called to tell Lynn that a policy had been put in place. Reporters no longer would be allowed to enter funeral homes without the family's permission.

One reporter impacted by Lynn was Alison Delsite, who worked for The Patriot-News in Harrisburg when Tom Snead murdered his children. She had acquired the legal papers surrounding his arrest for stalking. She had spoken to the disc jockey he stalked and had learned of her fears for the safety of Lynn's children. She called Lynn's parents' house the day after the murders to ask if Lynn wanted to comment. Until that moment, Lynn had been unaware of the stalking arrest. It was another example of her learning details from the media.

After the children's funeral, a friend of Lynn's called Alison and asked if they could meet. Lynn wanted to hear everything she knew about the disc jockey and the stalking incident. The trio went out for lunch. Alison and Lynn's friend talked about the incidents involving Tom. Alison recalls that Lynn "just sat there, catatonic."

Alison didn't write about that meeting, and for Lynn, that was the start of a trust. Alison, meanwhile, bided her time, but was gently persistent. "She just weighed on my mind so heavily," Alison said of Lynn. "So every couple of weeks I would call and check in. Then one day, she wanted to tell her story."

Alison said she looked at the piece she would write as "Lynn's story, not my story. It changed the way I looked at things. This is your story. I'm just the storyteller."

The first anniversary of the children's death was approaching. Paul was, as always, by Lynn's side. Alison took the couple through her story step by step. When Paul asked her to keep certain things out, she respected their wishes.

In many ways, Alison's gentle handling of Lynn changed her own life. She eventually left the newspaper and went to work for the Pennsylvania Commission on Crime and Delinquency and later for the Pennsylvania Coalition Against Domestic Violence. She began to work with Lynn, presenting seminars on how to get the story without traumatizing the victim.

Alison and Lynn went to statewide and national conferences to talk with advocates about the importance of the media and how to develop effective relationships. They also went into newspaper offices and college classrooms across Pennsylvania teaching reporters how to get a story without causing further harm to the victim. On her own, Lynn took their message to a national gathering of the Society of Professional Journalists.

Included in their message to reporters is a reminder that, initially, a victim is incapable of acting as a filter for herself. A compassionate reporter, they said, learns to be a filter for the victim, because not everything a traumatized victim blurts out should be fodder for the public. Their message reminds journalists that preparing a story might take minutes, but the effects on victims can last a lifetime. They also include a reminder that "anniversary" stories often re-victimize the victims.

After one such session at the Pittsburgh Post-Gazette, an editor said: "Most newsroom training sessions focus on the craft of journalism. Rarely do journalists get the chance to learn about the impact of their work from the people whose stories they tell, ordinary citizens whose real-life experiences with the media contain powerful lessons. (Lynn's) sobering comments and prescription for better reporting on victims offer a rarely heard but important perspective."

Among the questions Lynn asks journalists to ask themselves are the following:

- Why is this story legitimate?
- What do I really need to know to serve the public good?
- What additional harm might I be causing to vulnerable people?

- What alternatives can I consider as I go after information?
- What steps can I take to minimize the harm to people to whom I need to talk?
- What is the least intrusive way to contact those people?
- Can I use an intermediary to contact them?
- Can I talk with them at a later time when they might not be so vulnerable?
- Can I talk with them at a place and time that might be less intrusive?

In talking with journalists, Lynn also reminds them to consider their own needs. They have tough jobs which often find them wallowing in death, crime and unspeakable acts. How do they deal with vicarious trauma?

Vicarious trauma is a process that unfolds over time. It is not just an individual's response to one person, one story or one situation. It is the cumulative effect of contact with survivors of violence or disaster or people who are struggling. It is what happens over time as someone observes cruelty and loss or hears distressing stories, day after day, year after year.

Often, Lynn said, reporters will nod during this part of her presentation. Afterwards, some come up to discuss those feelings. Because they don't have the resources to debrief or work in an environment that has a support system in place, their emotional, physical and spiritual well-being can be endangered over time.

Nancy has shared her story with the Pennsylvania Newspaper and Broadcasters associations. Her goal is to one day educate law enforcement and others who have access to autopsy and crime scene photos about the impact of releasing those photos to the media.

Ironically, as both women forge ahead in their efforts to make a difference in the lives of crime victims, they have come to regard the media as a resource for spreading their message. While they acknowledge that journalists have a right, even an obligation, to report news about crime, they caution them to do so in a way that doesn't further harm the victims.

"The public has a right to know," Lynn said, "and the media needs to disseminate information to the community about the nature and extent of a crime in order to prevent crime and protect the community. However, it is hard for victims and their families to understand how personal, intimate details meet that goal. Providing those types of details without the family's permission is nothing more than sensationalism. While reporters have a legal right to publish certain information, they also have an ethical responsibility to go further and balance the potential for public good against the private harm to the victim."

Many families, Lynn said, want to share their stories or tell the media details about a loved one who has died. The key lies in asking. Permission and respect are of utmost importance.

"If you choose to interact with victims," Lynn said, "out of respect for them, you need to have an understanding of the effects of victimization. You must be sensitive to their needs and empathetic when dealing with them, and if you don't feel it, then fake it. If you can't feel it or fake it, then you should not be dealing with victims."

Like Lynn, Nancy has learned from the tragedy of her daughter's death. Victims, she said, must deal with the media on their own terms. Some will find the media to be allies, while others prefer to keep reporters at arm's length.

Those who don't want to talk might want to ask a friend or family member to handle requests from media. Those who wish to speak with the media can set rules, such as when and where the interview will take place and if any questions are off limits.

When one national television talk show asked Lynn to be part of a show, she asked for a day to decide. When the producer wouldn't give her that time, she simply said no.

Nancy also suggests that victims facing trials and other court appearances talk with local law enforcement or court officials before agreeing to be interviewed in order not to jeopardize the case.

When Nancy turns to the media now, it's on her terms. She uses the media to promote her causes: the fight against domestic violence and her determination to build Randi's House of Angels, a place for children whose lives are impacted by domestic violence.

In 2010, when Nancy told her story to a magazine reporter, she made her reasons for the interview clear.

"I just want so much for the women out there – and there are men, too – who walk around in silence, behind closed doors, protecting their abusers, like I did, to know that they can make a difference," she told the reporter. "It starts with them. They have to want to change. And that's where I will concentrate my efforts for probably the rest of my life. I miss Randi every minute of my life, but if this wouldn't have happened, I wouldn't be helping others."

Chapter 10

Forgiveness

A wave of nausea washed over Nancy Chavez when she retrieved her mail one day in November 2004. In her hands she found a letter from a Pennsylvania state prison. It was from Brian Trimble, the man who had married her daughter in a beautiful Catholic ceremony and then planned her murder three years later.

Nancy's initial inclination was to leave the contents in the envelope. Perhaps in anticipation, Trimble had written on the back, "Please read this letter Nancy."

Nancy was awash in stress and fear. She flashed back to the day of her daughter's funeral. She had sat in church, holding Brian's hand, concerned for his welfare. She saw him as a fragile young widower that day, and Nancy wanted to shield him from the hurt that buffeted her. Now she saw him as the architect of her daughter's murder.

Although it was late, Nancy called her sister, crying. She held the envelope. Should she open it? Just touching it made her feel dirty because Brian Trimble's hands had held it.

Nancy battled with herself. She and her sister discussed her choices. If she didn't read it, she might regret it later. If she did, she was opening herself to Brian's lies and attempts at manipulation. Deep down, Nancy knew that if she left the letter unopened, the contents would haunt her. So she pulled out the letter and found Brain's pathetic attempt to explain why he had decided to kill Randi.

It read:

> Dear Nancy,
> This is the most difficult thing I have ever had to write. I know you are angry, and hurt, but I thought you had the right to know what was going through my mind, when I made the most horrible mistake of my life. This letter is not intended to justify my actions, as there is no excuse for what I did. I just want to try to help you understand.
> First, Randi and I had a very difficult marriage. There was no infidelity, or lack of trust, just arguing. Years of arguing. The only time we were really at peace was when other people were around and then it was just an act. At the time, I thought Randi was the cause of our problems, but that is not the case. The problems were mostly caused by me. I was depressed, and frustrated by our arguments, and my state of mind led to further arguments. It got to the point where I wanted a divorce. I thought of telling her this for a very long time, but I was not man enough to talk to her about it. I was scared of what my future would hold, and I loved (still love) Randi very much. I could not bring myself to look her in the eye, and tell her I wanted a divorce. I did not know what to do. For a long time, I was miserable, and I even attempted to commit suicide several times. In retrospect, it would have been better had I succeeded, as Randi would still be with you. I began to discuss my problems with my coworker Blaine. As I talked more to him, he suggested eliminating Randi as a means to solve my problems. At first, I

was appalled, but as months went by his rhetoric, combined with my depression began to make the idea attractive. I was so focused on myself, I didn't think of how it would affect others. I didn't think of you, your family, or my family. I know we all love Randi very much. After it was done, I also realized that I was wrong about how it would affect me as well. Starting on Jan. 10, 2003 and to this minute, I regret, and am remorseful for what I have done. I think of Randi every day, and I miss her very much. I still love her very much, and I love you and your family as well. I know, nothing I say can undo my actions, but I would if I could, and it has nothing to do with my incarceration. I deserve to be jailed (at the least) for what I have done. I pray every day for forgiveness from God, and I will never stop. I hope you find it in your heart to forgive me as well, but I understand if you cannot. Please know that Randi means everything to me, even now. I love her very much, and I love you as well. If you want to correspond with me, I would be honored. I will do my best to answer any questions you may have. I will do anything you ask of me always. I pray you understand, although what I did is the worst thing I could have done. I love you and God bless.

Love, Brian

Forgive him? Correspond with him? Had Brian Trimble gone mad? Did he honestly not understand what he had done to Nancy when he took the life of her only daughter? Forgive him? It wasn't her job. "I don't believe it's my role to forgive them. The person who could forgive Brian would be Randi, and she's not here," Nancy said.

To this day, Nancy regards that letter with disgust. It seems to her as if Brian tried to explain why he thought Randi deserved to be killed.

Nancy didn't respond to the letter, but her brother-in-law did. Mike Wilson, in his role as Randi's attorney, sent Brian legal papers on Nov. 23, 2004. He included a letter in which he asked Brian to stop writing to Nancy and told him he would not be hearing from him again.

After explaining that he was aware of how Brian had manipulated Randi's family and friends, as well as law enforcement, Wilson ended by saying: "At this point, I believe it is best if you just left us alone and went on with your time. Your betrayal of us is complete and permanent. We treated you with the best of our emotions and feelings and you simply spat on us and held us, along with Randi, in your private world of contempt. Neither Randi nor our family ever did anything to you to remotely deserve this – and you know it."

Perhaps Brian stewed over this. Maybe he thought time would heal the wounds, because on Jan. 11, 2011, he wrote Nancy another letter, churning up all the emotions his first letter had caused.

His second letter was shorter, but once again he asked for forgiveness.

He wrote:

> Dear Nancy,
> I know that I am the last person in the world you want to hear from, but I feel that I need to offer you some explanation, so that you may get some closure. I am no longer fighting my case in court, so there is no longer a need to hide the truth.
> I want to begin by telling you that I love Randi. I always have, and I always will. There were problems in our relationship that neither of us knew how to handle, and that combined with my self-centeredness, and immaturity led to what happened.
> Our relationship was very much bipolar. It was either very good, or very bad, with little room in between. I know we loved each other, but we were not good at communicating. Both of us kept secrets

from one another, and we developed resentment towards one another.

I have always felt that she resented me for not finishing college, and not being motivated. I wish I could have told her that I didn't like myself for the very same reasons. I knew I could do so much more, but after we were married, it felt like there was never time.

I resented her for her thriftiness, I appreciate the need to save money but have never been very good at it. She was the opposite. She had difficulty letting go of a single dollar, and we were never able to come to a compromise. I believe it was my frustration at these things and others that led to her death. I know it was a horrible thing, and I regretted her death the moment it happened. If I could, I would change places with her in a heartbeat.

I ask only that you try to find it in your heart to forgive me. I am not asking that you forget, or that you trust me, only that you forgive. Please know that I love you too, as the mother I wish I had. You were always hard on me, and I think that is what I needed. I thank you for that, even though I was very intimidated by you. I know you are a good woman, and so was Randi.

I don't know if this [is] enough of an explanation for you, but I hope it is. If not, I will be happy to answer any questions you may have, and if there is anything I can do to help you, please let me know. I know it doesn't change anything, but I am sorry. Please forgive me.

Love, Brian

Nancy still insists it is not her place to forgive Brian or Blaine Norris. Weaving the loss of their children into their lives is a journey, Lynn and Nancy say. Because Lynn's children were murdered a decade before Randi, she has traveled farther on that journey. Although Nancy is not ready to forgive, she has reached a point where she has thought about it.

"I remember the exact date I experienced a feeling of need to one day consider forgiving the two people who killed Randi," she said. "Every Friday morning, I extend my drive to work so that I can listen to 'StoryCorps' [on NPR], a project that records conversations between loved ones and friends.

"On May 11, 2011, there was a story about a mother forgiving her son's killer. I placed myself in the mother's shoes as she talked about her son and how the murder occurred. She went into Stillwater Prison [in Minnesota] and talked to the grown man who had murdered her son. She said that he became human and she hugged him. After she left, she realized that all the anger and animosity and all the stuff she had in her for more than 12 years was over. She had forgiven him.

"That mother's story never left me. It gave me something to think about. Perhaps one day I will also experience what she had longed for."

That day isn't here, but Nancy no longer says never.

Currently, she walks a fine line, carrying her hate while attempting to avoid obsession.

"I decided from the beginning that I couldn't become obsessed about Brian Trimble or Blaine Norris," she said. "They took everything. They took my entire life. But I have to move forward. I can be very, very angry. I am angry, and I do hate them, but I don't want to become obsessed by it. I don't want them to know how much I suffer."

Although Nancy loves her job and stays busy at work, she suffers the loss of Randi every day. "When I walk out of work, I'm the loneliest person," she said. "My home is my safe haven, where I can be surrounded by pictures and memories of Randi."

Nancy still vividly recalls sitting in a small courtroom on September 29, 2003. As she witnessed the court proceedings that day, she couldn't help but think that in earlier times she could have watched as both men were lynched on the square.

If she had never given much thought to the death penalty, losing her daughter changed that. In the months that followed, she examined the death penalty from all sides, alone and with her priest. Today, Nancy supports the death penalty. While Brian and Blaine are behind bars for the rest of their lives, they are, at least, alive. Randi is not.

"Shame on me for not being against the death penalty," Nancy said. "People don't know until it happens to them."

Over the years, she has discussed crime and punishment, feelings and emotions with Lynn in a way that, perhaps, only the mother of a murdered child could understand.

"Lynn probably doesn't know this, but she's my mentor," Nancy said.

In some ways, Lynn said, she thinks Nancy has had the harder road. Lynn's ex-husband killed himself immediately after killing their children. While Lynn and Paul were told to stay in the area and were interviewed at the local police department after her children were buried, that was it. No court proceedings, letters from prison, appeals or commutations loomed in her future.

But there's a downside to that. Crime victims are generally assigned an advocate, someone employed by the district attorney's office to explain their rights, walk them through the proceedings, assist in filing a claim for expenses incurred as a result of the crime, support their interests and listen. Because Lynn didn't have an offender in "the system," she wasn't assigned an advocate. She had to try to make sense of what was happening on her own.

Lynn was angry. She dreamt repeatedly of killing Tom Snead with guns, knives and by pulling his organs out of his body with her bare hands. Each time she woke, she found herself frightened and shaking because Tom had been in her dreams and she had felt capable of murder while she slept. She carried hate and a need for revenge and had no place to take those feelings.

After the murders of her children, she wanted to strike out. "If Tom were alive and I had access to him, I think I may have been capable of killing him," she said.

Like his daughter, Ed Monk feels that if Tom had lived, he could have killed him. "I'm a friendly guy. I could have taken Tom for a ride and just lost him," he said.

Instead, he had to be content with fantasies of going to the cemetery and blowing up Tom's grave.

Tom may be gone, but Lynn's father still harbors his hatred. "I don't see how a person could forgive," he said.

For a long time, Lynn didn't either, but deep down, she said, "I always knew I would need to forgive Tom. In the beginning, I would joke that when I am on my death bed and have about five seconds left, then I'll forgive. I'll slide that in, right at the end."

In about 2002, eight years after Jen and Dave's murders, Lynn spoke at a national conference about her journey as a victim of crime. "After I shared my story, a woman approached and indicated that we had something in common, the loss of a child. It has always been easy for me to talk with other parents whose children have been murdered. There is this silent acknowledgment of acceptance between us. We are part of that club that no one wants to be a member of. We don't know exactly what the other has gone through, but we each understand the intensity of the pain and the grief.

"We talked about 15 minutes, and my only thought was, 'It's too soon for her to be attending a conference like this.' Through her sobbing, I could barely understand what she was trying to share with me about her son and what had happened and how she felt. Her emotions were so raw that I simply assumed that the murder was fairly recent.

"During the conversation, she made reference to a year, and I said, 'Oh, Jen and Dave were born in the '80s, too.' She corrected me and said her child hadn't been born in the '80s, he had been murdered in the '80s. It had been 20 years since her son was murdered.

"That was an epiphany for me, a defining moment. It had been around eight years since Jen and Dave died. I knew at that moment that I couldn't be that woman in another 12 years. While her emotions flowed freely, mine were a weight on my chest, settled into a chronic ache in my heart, and wedged in my stomach with a whole lot of sadness and emptiness stored in my eyes and my soul. My ex-husband had murdered his own children, ruined my life and caused incredible heartache for many. I was functioning just fine, but I was struggling with the pain and sadness and still had occasional thoughts of suicide.

The offender, my ex, had made my life miserable for the 10 years we were married, and tore my world apart by killing Jen and Dave. And eight years after their murder, in essence, he was continuing to control my physical and emotional well-being. The anger was sucking the energy out of me. I was going to self-destruct. It had to stop. I made a decision that day that I wouldn't allow him to ruin the rest of my life."

Once she made that decision, 10 years after losing her children, she found a huge weight had been lifted off her shoulders.

As a result of that encounter, Lynn began to think seriously about forgiveness.

Forgive the monster who murdered her children? Forgive the man they called Daddy who stole their futures?

Over the years, Lynn and Paul have come to realize that Tom Snead was mentally ill. His obsession with a disc jockey, his assertion that he was going to marry Celine Dion, his masquerading as a clergyman to visit hospitals were all signs of his break with reality.

Forgiveness, Lynn realized, has absolutely nothing to do with forgetting.

"I started by looking in Webster's Dictionary, because I wasn't quite sure what forgiveness meant. 'To excuse for an offense; to release the liability for or penalty entailed by an offense.' That didn't quite fit my feelings or needs. So I looked again. 'To renounce (give up or disown) anger or resentment against.' Close, but still not quite what I needed.

"So I decided to write my own definition of forgiveness: An empowering act to rid oneself of the rage and anger caused by the heinous, selfish act of another. This type of forgiveness may allow one to transcend all of the energy it takes to harbor the anger and hatred, and provides the ability to channel energy into more constructive, positive things."

In disowning her anger and resentment, Lynn handed everything over to God. Let Him be the judge. And although Lynn has forgiven, she will carry the pain of her loss until the day she dies.

While this worked for her, she is quick to say that no one should tell a crime victim to forgive. Each person has the right to act in his or her own way. "They need to do what they need to do to survive and move forward," Lynn said. "Until we walk in their shoes, we have no right to suggest, second-guess or tell them if and when they need to forgive. If and when it is time, they will know it and act on it."

Chapter 11

Lynn's Deep Rooted Need to Make a Difference

Lynn knew that her ex-husband was odd. She had lived with the man and endured his abuse. She knew he was manipulative. But never in her worst nightmares did she think he would harm their children.

Even a judge had reinforced that belief. When she went into court seeking supervised visitation for her children, the judge told her, "Just because he hits you, Mother, it doesn't mean he would hurt his children."

So Lynn was happy for her children that Christmas in 1994. No matter how odd Tom Snead was, his children loved him. He said he would be taking them out to Christmas Eve dinner. In the morning, there would be gifts. The children said good-bye to Lynn with smiles on their faces.

It was only after Tom slaughtered the children that Lynn learned he had been arrested a month earlier for stalking and harassing a disc jockey in a neighboring county.

Beginning in the early part of 1994, Tom had repeatedly made dedications to be read on the radio show, "Lights Out," which was broadcast on a station in Lancaster County.

The show's disc jockey, who used the on-air name of Deb Friday, said Tom's initial dedication was to Jennifer. His words were so touching that Deb featured it on the opening of her show. Tom had faxed:

"To little Jennifer in Colonial Park, whose heart shines so very bright.

Whose eyes sparkle like the brightest stars on a dark clear night.

Oh my, when she plays her clarinet, I run for cover.

She laughs, she giggles, she knows I always come back for I do very, very much love her."

Soon after, he faxed a dedication to both of his children:

"Sometimes I don't tell you kids how much I love you with all of my heart and I know I should. You're the greatest kids a dad could have."

Often the dedications were for a "pretty Canadian woman." Later, people would discover the Canadian lady, the one Tom intended to marry, was singer Celine Dion. He wrote:

"My pretty Canadian lady so very far away, it's just another morning, just another day.

I've thought about you and I've thought about us, are you playing with me or are you serious...

I've been hurt too much in this lonely life. I've lost my children and been cut by an ex-wife.

Is this what you'll do, just another game.

I guess I sound sorry for I've no one else to blame."

Other times, his messages were nasty. He faxed one for Sara in Harrisburg that read, "I like your taste in music, but your art work is weird and so are you. Bye!"

Deb knew the same man was sending the faxes because the phone number of his fax machine was printed across the top of each sheet of paper. However, no one at the station knew his last name. They knew him only as "Tom from Linglestown," which is how he signed notes he included with his requests to Deb.

Tom seemed to become more and more drawn into the radio show. He sent the disc jockey a letter containing $180 in cash and asking her to send roses to a "very special person ... bet you can't guess who." Deb had no idea where he wanted those roses to go.

Then, on September 3, 1994, in a fit of anger at the disc jockey for not playing his dedications, he smashed the windshield of her car and left her a note on the back of a bank receipt, saying "You're nothing but a Liar, Drop Dead!"

The incident left the disc jockey shaken. The radio station was in a rather isolated rural location, and she worked until midnight. Somehow Tom knew what car was hers, while she had no idea what he looked like.

She called the police immediately and told the officer who responded that she thought her windshield had been broken by the man who had been sending the faxes. She felt that the officer didn't show much concern.

A few weeks later, Deb received flowers, apparently as an apology, but they had no message and no name attached. She phoned the florist to ask who had sent them. Tom Snead. She immediately phoned the police and gave them the name. Police then told her that was the name associated with the bank receipt left on her windshield.

Deb and her co-workers took the incident very seriously. Her co-workers followed her home for weeks to ensure her safety. She bought a car phone, went on a strength-training program, and changed her lifestyle because she was fearful of this man whose face she had never seen.

"I took him as a lonely, bitter, troubled person who was using me (and the show) to be heard," Deb said. "He certainly wasn't the only unstable person my co-workers and I talked to during the show, but the frequency of his faxes and calls raised a red flag."

Deb said she called state police to check on the status of the case, but they downplayed her concern. She told them she feared for the man's children as he was using Jennifer to call the radio station and request dedications of nasty break-up songs he wanted the disc jockey to play for certain women.

Overall, his actions and comments prompted the disc jockey, who was just 24 at the time, to write to the state police. In a letter dated December 13, 1994, she wrote: "I feel it is imperative that you check Thomas Snead's background for previous acts of violence and misconduct… I continue to worry about myself, as well as other women who may have been, or will be, harassed or victimized by Mr. Snead. Obviously something is not right with this man."

In addition to the letter, she sent police copies of the faxes he had sent.

Tom Snead confessed during an interview with the state police and was subsequently charged with stalking and harassment on December 7th. He was due to appear in court in January 1995.

None of this information reached Lynn.

Reporter Alison Delsite shared this information with Lynn in the days immediately after Jen and Dave's deaths. In her grief, Lynn was horrified. How could she, who had primary custody of their two children, be unaware of Tom's arrest? Shouldn't somebody have been looking out for the well-being of her children?

Sheri Rowe, a friend of Lynn's, called The Pennsylvania Coalition Against Domestic Violence and shared Lynn's concerns with Judy Yupcavage, who, at that time, was the public policy and information manager. A meeting grew from that call.

Judy recalls the day the women met. Lynn, she said, "was frail and pale and sunken and lifeless. You could tell she was just barely holding it together."

The women explored the idea of a law and asked the Public Interest Resource Center of Widener University School of Law to research and draft proposed legislation. They devised a bill that would make it possible for parents in custody situations to be notified if the other parent is charged with a crime. They approached state Senator Jeffrey Piccola and asked if he would sponsor the bill. He jumped on board and quickly found about 25 senators to co-sponsor the bill.

The bill was introduced in February 1996 during a news conference, with Lynn present. "This was my very first time at a news conference," Lynn recalled, "and I was petrified, especially with all of the media there. Senator Piccola introduced the bill, shared the history and importance of it, and asked for swift and immediate passage. Listening to the senator talk about Jen and Dave with his voice cracking and his eyes tearful was taking its toll on me; I was afraid I might collapse.

"Emotions were extremely high in the room, and when it was my turn to talk, I was holding on to the podium so tightly that my fingers started to ache. I read a prepared statement pleading for support to help protect our children, and then for the first time in public, I spoke to Jen and Dave through tears: 'Jen and Dave, because of you, I am stronger than I ever thought I could be and stronger than I ever wanted to be. Your entire life was stolen from you, and I'd give anything in the world to change the past. I know that yesterday is gone forever. But, I promise I will do everything I can to prevent this from happening to other children. I miss you and love you with all of my heart.'"

Despite the emotion of that introduction, Morgan Plant, the lobbyist for the coalition, said several members of the state Legislature, as well as policy makers, had privately questioned the need for such a law. Lynn challenged them to "ask me to my face." And so she was invited to testify before the Senate Judiciary Committee.

"She went in with this little frail voice, and she sat in front of the committee and she was shaking," Judy recalled.

Lynn was asking for a law that would let the other parent know if there had been an arrest. Then, the parent could take what he or she had learned into court and ask the judge for a custody modification.

Lynn faced the table of senators and said, "Our children need and deserve to be protected and, if our current custody laws cannot afford this protection, they need to be changed. If, by making this change, we save one life, our efforts have been successful. We need to continue to take steps towards protecting the most cherished and vulnerable people in the world, our children."

After she spoke, no one asked any questions. The committee voted unanimously to move the bill forward. The entire Senate then passed the bill and sent it to the House, where it sat until that group reconvened in October.

"Lynn really did set aside all of her grief to do this," Judy Yupcavage said. "It wasn't going to help her. It wasn't going to bring back her kids."

The law, which came to be known as Jen and Dave's Law, is remembered as the fastest piece of legislation ever to work its way through the state's Legislature.

"In an extremely rare gesture, I was invited onto the House floor to witness the passage of this legislation," Lynn said. "I was overwhelmed, intimidated, and still painfully shy, and said no, thank you. I can still recall Morgan Plant, the lobbyist, taking my arm and saying, 'I wasn't asking. This is history in the making, and you are going to be there.' And I'm glad I was there."

The Speaker of the House welcomed Lynn, and the legislation was dedicated to the memory of her children. The date was October 1 – the first day of Domestic Violence Awareness Month. Then the House floor became quiet, which is extremely unusual, and everyone watched the vote board. Green lights came on next to the name of every single representative. The final vote was unanimous, 201-0. At the conclusion, Lynn received a standing ovation.

"To this day, I still don't think I fully understand the amount of time and effort and the number of people who got behind this bill to guide it to passage," Lynn said. "I only knew how grateful I was."

Jen and Dave's Law was signed by Governor Tom Ridge in November 1996. Pennsylvania had established the nation's first automated system that enables a parent or guardian in a child custody arrangement to learn if the other parent or guardian has been charged with specific criminal offenses in the state.

A press conference was planned for a public signing by the governor, and Lynn was asked to sit beside Ridge while he signed Jen and Dave's Law. With them were those who had worked to make the law a reality, along with Lynn's family, friends, and about 10 of Jen and Dave's friends.

At one point during the ceremony, the governor leaned over and began asking Lynn questions about the Victims Compensation Program, which she had recently agreed to help streamline. "I thought to myself, 'This is Jen and Dave's day. I don't want to think about anything else but this moment.' To this day, I still can't believe that I reached over, patted his forearm and said, 'Don't worry about it; I'll take care of it.' He nodded, smiled and said, 'I'm sure you will.'

It was such a bittersweet day.

"One personal moment that my family still laughs about occurred after the signing," Lynn said. "Pictures were being taken, and in one shot, all of my family members had their picture taken with the governor. Other than a handshake, people are not supposed to touch the governor.

"Well, here's my dad, a warm, outgoing man in his 70's, who was very touched by the signing, and everyone is his buddy and everything is a 'good deal.' He walks up to the governor, is shaking his hand and with the other hand begins to pat him on the back repeatedly. The pats are hard enough that the governor was moving forward with each pat. My dad was saying, 'Thanks a lot, buddy, good deal, you did a great job.' All the while the governor's head is going back and forth. I was later told that he was making security somewhat nervous. We could see the headlines, 'Jen and Dave's grandfather assaults governor.'"

Lynn might have scored a victory and enjoyed a chuckle that day, but she was still a broken woman.

Judy Yupcavage was so impressed by Lynn that she nominated her for the National Crime Victims' Service Award.

Although she didn't win that year (she would win the award in 2004), she received a letter of commendation.

In her nominating letter, Judy wrote, "During the past three years, I've watched Lynn mourn for her children, yet find strength in knowing her efforts could make a difference in the lives of other children. I've seen the anguish in her eyes as well as the determination of her spirit. Slowly, but very surely, she began her journey back from grief by becoming an advocate for battered women and their children and a champion for Jen and Dave's Law."

From somewhere deep inside, Lynn drew on a strength she hadn't known she possessed. At some point in her grieving, she reached a place where she knew she no longer wanted to simply exist. Jen and Dave had been shortchanged, and Lynn wanted to make their mark for them.

"What would they think of me if I didn't value my own life?" Lynn asked herself. "In my mind, I needed to make up for what they would have offered. I know that I'm not going to fix or change the world, but while I'm here, I'm going to make a difference."

Since that epiphany, she has had opportunities to address the media, clergy, legislators, journalism students, seminarians, crime victims, advocates, inmates, funeral directors, medical practitioners, the community and even a coalition whose mission is to abolish the death penalty. She has been a keynote speaker at conferences and trainings across the nation.

"I put myself out there in hopes that one person can pick up a valuable piece of information that may help them personally or help them in gaining a new perspective on crime victims," she said.

The deaths of Lynn's children on Christmas day touched the community, as well. People wanted to do something; they wanted to help in some way. With the help of Ken Beard, the principal of North Side Elementary School, which the children had attended, Lynn established a memorial fund. More than $9,000 was raised and used to buy library books, soccer goals, computer software, music for the chorus, two violins for needy children, media material relating to family dynamics and land-scaping, which included the "Jen and Dave Memorial Garden," designed by Lynn's friend Ruth Brown. They also planted two trees in front of the school in the children's memory.

The state agency where Lynn worked joined with the Public School Employees' Retirement System, where Lynn's sister worked, and collected a significant contribution for the Jen and Dave Fund. Lynn and her sister also held a small holiday drive for the Harrisburg YWCA in December 1995. Lynn had been hoping for a carload of gifts. Instead, they gathered several truckloads of children's clothes and toys, along with Christmas gifts and money to help support the women and children housed at the YWCA.

Lynn was overwhelmed and grateful for the concern, support, kindness and generosity of the community.

In the spring of 1995, Paul dragged Lynn onto a golf course, where, for a brief moment, she felt as though Jen and Dave were surrounding her. "I said to Paul, 'How hard do you think it could be to organize a golf tournament in memory of Jen and Dave?'"

Five months later, with an incredible group of volunteers, the 1st Annual Jen and Dave Memorial Golf Tournament was held, raising $9,000, well above the $2,500 goal. Community members and businesses donated thousands of dollars of merchandise. The following year, a silent auction was added to the golf tournament. The total take was $17,000. Each year, the event exceeded Lynn's expectations.

The fifth and final golf tournament and silent auction was held in 2001 and raised more than $50,000, bringing the cumulative total to more than $160,000. Proceeds went to support the Pennsylvania Coalition Against Domestic Violence, the Harrisburg YWCA and ParentWorks, an organization dedicated to helping individuals improve their parenting skills.

These early efforts, undertaken during a time of immense grieving, offered comfort. Lynn wanted to educate parents about domestic violence and its effects, including the effects on children who witness abuse but might not be targets themselves. She wanted to share with mothers what she didn't realize, that if he's capable of hurting you, he's capable of hurting the kids. There is no line an abuser will not cross.

In the fall of 1995, Lynn went through 58 hours of counselor advocacy training to become a volunteer at the YWCA of Harrisburg, which provides services to victims of domestic violence and sexual assault. She volunteered to take hot line calls as well as to work with children while their mothers went to individual or group counseling.

Her hotline and children's support group work was short-lived. In December of 1995, she had a hot line call from a mother of two children whose husband was abusive and thought he was God. Unbelievably, her children's names were Jen and Dave.

"I listened for two hours about the abuse, harassment and how he would hold her down and make the kids hit her in the face," Lynn said. "I explained the Protection from Abuse Order process and who she should contact and talked about a safety plan. I was trained to help women find resources within themselves and within the community. What I really wanted to tell her was what had happened to me. My children's names are Jen and Dave, too, and I wanted to tell her to take her kids and run. None of that was appropriate.

"That same week, I helped an experienced volunteer with the children's support group. I watched how a child mimicked to her baby doll the harsh words of her parent. I then watched as another child acted out with puppets what the child was witnessing in her own home.

"Between the hot line calls and the children's support group, I quickly realized, I couldn't do this work. Initially, I thought I was a failure. I went through all of that training and barely made it a month. I wasn't ready. I couldn't set healthy boundaries for myself. I couldn't help myself from being emotionally invested. I eventually realized that I wasn't a failure. I was a grieving mess who hadn't even made it to the first anniversary of Jen and Dave's death."

In 1996, the YWCA and others nominated Lynn to receive the Regaining One's Self-Esteem Award. The R.O.S.E. Fund is a national nonprofit organization committed to ending violence against women and assisting women survivors of violence to regain their self-esteem. The award was created to recognize a woman survivor who is a role model and an inspiration to other women survivors of violence, who has advanced the opportunities for other women survivors of violence, and whose work with victims has resulted in considerable positive change and achievement on a regional or national level.

Lynn was the second recipient of this prestigious award. The YWCA received a monetary award, which was matched by the Whitaker Foundation. It provided an indoor play area in the domestic violence shelter called Jen and Dave's Place. The foundation flew Lynn and Paul to Boston to the annual gala to receive the award from Theresa Heinz and Robert Kraft, owner of the New England Patriots football team.

Lynn remembers this as a classy black-tie event. But just like the bill-signing with the governor, it would contain its lighter moment.

Paul and Lynn were sitting at a small table talking before the dinner began. Paul was reading the events program. "There was," Lynn recalled, "a candle in the middle of our table, and we noticed tiny pieces of ash begin to float above us. Paul's program had caught fire, and he had to take his drink and napkin to douse it. I was horrified. I can only imagine what others thought. There was a huge hole in the middle of his program. I didn't think it was funny at the time, but later always joked about how Paul lit up the room."

If that wasn't excitement enough, Lynn met Drew Bledsoe, quarterback for the Patriots, a strong supporter of raising awareness about domestic violence.

But Lynn was about to tackle another challenge.

When Lynn buried her children, she paid just over $8,000 in funeral and burial expenses from her savings account, wiping out what it had taken her 10 years to save. She turned to the Crime Victims Compensation Program for reimbursement in

January of 1995. This is a state program that was established
in 1976 to help victims of crime with the financial impact. The
program was able to reimburse Lynn for a significant portion
of the funeral and burial expenses, as well as the cost of her
counseling.

Nine months later, a check arrived in the mail. Lynn was
grateful for the money, but the wait, shorter than what most
victims faced, seemed totally unacceptable.

"I was fortunate that I had $8,000 in my savings and Paul,
who insisted on helping me to cover my counseling fees," Lynn
said. "But when I thought about it, I knew most people probably didn't have that money in their savings or friends or family
to help pay other expenses. In a way, the program, as it existed,
was revictimizing the crime victim."

In April of 1996 Governor Tom Ridge recognized Lynn's
legislative and fund-raising efforts by appointing her to the
state's Victims' Services Advisory Committee. The purpose of
VSAC is to serve in an advisory capacity to the Pennsylvania
Commission on Crime and Delinquency and to assure that the
voices, needs and perspectives of crime victims or survivors
will be considered in the development of services, service standards, policies, funding priorities, legislation and outcomes.

Lynn had been working at the Department of Labor and
Industry as a division chief in the Bureau of Worker and
Community Right to Know, which helps inform individuals
about the chemicals they are exposed to at their workplaces
and about chemicals being emitted into the environment.

She had been at Labor and Industry for 18 years, but the
work now seemed less important to her. Through her new
appointment, she was given the opportunity to work with
Pennsylvania's Victims Compensation Assistance Program
(VCAP) on a part-time basis to assist in streamlining the
operation. In April of 1997, she accepted a full-time job with
the Office of Victims' Services, and in August of 1998 accepted
the position of manager of VCAP. Lynn, no doubt, had the
expertise for the job. She had been dubbed an efficiency expert
by her peers.

"I had never been in such a challenging, yet rewarding, position. I had been through the compensation process myself, as a claimant, and was well aware of the amount of time it took to get a claim through the process," Lynn said.

As Lynn began to unpeel the layers, she soon discovered that Pennsylvania had one of the worst programs in the nation. It was known as one of the best-kept secrets in Pennsylvania, and the decisions being made on claims were termed by the media as "penurious and capricious." The program was unresponsive to the needs of crime victims.

There was a large pot of money that was supposed to reimburse crime victims for expenses that resulted from their victimization, such as medical bills, lost wages and funeral costs, yet most victims didn't know it existed.

Lynn's job, as she saw it, was to reduce the red tape faced by victims, spread the word about the program, and build strong partnerships throughout the state. Also key was educating those working in the system not to judge victims based on their life circumstances. Society is diverse, with people from all walks of life being dealt life experiences. The bottom line is that no one deserves to be a victim of crime. Lynn's mission was to ensure that decisions were made based on facts, not personal morals or assumptions.

Today, because of partnerships created all over the state and a dedicated and motivated staff, the program has become focused on victims' services. Under Lynn's leadership, obtaining compensation is easier, faster and victim-centered. Since she arrived, claims have increased by 321 percent.

The claim backlog, which topped 1,200 when she started, was eliminated, and processing time was cut by more than 20 weeks. Her success in streamlining the program involved directing and overseeing the design and implementation of a state-of-the-art automated claims processing system that was named for her son – Dependable Access for Victim's Expenses, or DAVE.

In her job, Lynn has experienced many days that leave her exhausted. One of those came after the 9/11 terrorist attacks.

Flight 93, which had been aiming for a target in Washington, D.C., crashed in an open field in Pennsylvania.

"Our staff, Bill, Ed, Regina, and I, were honored to partner with Mary Achilles, Pennsylvania's victim advocate at the time, to meet with the family members of the Flight 93 victims several days after the 9/11 terrorist attack," Lynn said. "I was scared," Lynn said. "In fact, I didn't want to go. I just wanted to stay in my safe little home, in Paul's arms, and watch everything unfold from my television. I didn't think I could handle it, professionally or personally. However, I did go, and we were at a lodge and there were approximately 100 grief-stricken family members from Flight 93.

There were many different agencies on-site helping with a variety of needs. Our role was to provide information on Victim's Compensation to help families understand about the program and that payments could be considered for funeral/burial costs, future counseling, etc.

"In a room full of grief, one experienced the raw trauma, shock, sobbing, anger, disbelief, and more. I had worked with homicide survivors, but never immediately following the death or in such a wide-scale tragedy. This was a turning point for me. I had talked with other victims who have lost loved ones, but I was afraid that I wouldn't be able to do my job and this event would bring back all of the pain, devastation, and helplessness experienced from Jen and Dave's murder. It didn't.

"Obviously, it was heart-wrenching, and I can actually recall a moment where I thought, 'For each of them, this is not the hardest part. … Next week, next month, next year will be just as hard, if not harder.' It was a defining moment, because I could actually separate my pain from others'. This event had absolutely nothing to do with Jen and Dave. I knew what the people in the room were going through, and I could listen, ask questions about their loved ones and listen some more. I had something to offer, and it wasn't about me."

One of the things advocates are taught is not to disclose to victims events from their own lives. The families of the Flight

93 victims may have found Lynn compassionate and understanding, but they had no idea why.

Lynn recalls only two times out of hundreds that she crossed the line and shared her story.

"The first occurred when a staff member transferred a call to me from a woman who was devastated about the murder of her daughter and angry because our program would not pay for counseling. In the 1990s, we only paid for counseling for the parents if the child lived with the parents. So, parents whose children were in college or living on their own when they were murdered were not eligible. (The law has since been changed.)

"The call was transferred because there was a concern that this woman was suicidal. I took the call and listened as she described the murder and said she didn't want to live anymore. I asked her to talk a little more about that and gently prodded to see if she had a plan as to how she would end her life. She broke down sobbing, not knowing if she had anything to live for. The pain was unbearable, and she didn't know how she would ever survive the death of her only daughter.

"I listened and validated her feelings and said those seven words that you are trained not to say, 'I understand what you are going through,' and followed up by sharing my story, a little of my journey, the importance of therapy and my certainty that she wasn't alone. I could feel a sense of relief through the phone. Ten-plus years later, we still chat.

"The second instance involved a homicide case in which the claim was denied. Essentially, the person is told he or she has the right to appeal the decision and tell the program why he or she thinks the decision we made is not correct. If our decision is upheld, the person has a right to request a hearing. Prior to holding a formal hearing, in cases of homicide, the program may offer a 'consultative session.'

"During a consultative session, a facilitator brings together program staff and the person who filed the claim (often a parent) to discuss the details of the decision and offer the person an opportunity to share whatever he or she feels is important.

Our decisions are based on information gleaned from police reports, and oftentimes it includes information that a parent is not aware of, such as the child was involved in illegal activity at the time that was related to his or her death.

"We were sitting in a small room, a mother and her close friend, Bonnie Bechtel a staff person and me, and the facilitator, Alberta James. We explained why we denied the claim. The mother was so angry about our decision that she stood up and leaned over the table. She was probably three times my size and was in my space, yelling that I was nothing more than a bureaucrat and that I didn't have a clue, sitting in my cozy office in Harrisburg, what it was like to have a child murdered and to be left with nothing but 'missed moments.'

"I was shaking and had to excuse myself from the room. I pulled it together, went back in the room and asked if she was finished. Then I said it was my turn to talk, and I told her about my children's murders. Her demeanor changed in seconds. We discussed the claim, and our children, and she said she was grateful we had met with her.

"It certainly shouldn't be the norm. But in these cases, it was the right thing to do."

The changes in how Pennsylvania treats its crime victims and survivors are a tribute to Lynn, and through her, to Jen and Dave.

"I'm proud of how staff and so many stakeholders across the state have worked together to make a difference in the lives of crime victims," Lynn said. "Pennsylvania is now touted as one of the best programs in the nation. Our focus is to remember that every piece of paper is not just a piece of paper. It is a part of a victim's journey, and providing quality services and resources is our responsibility."

Victims may be grateful for the funds that reimburse them, but it takes a special person to make the people who pay into the fund understand its importance. Lynn did just that in May 2006, when she walked into the imposing fortress that is the State Correctional Institution at Huntingdon. She had been invited to go behind barbed-wire-topped walls, to speak at the second Day of Responsibility, sponsored by the Pennsylvania Lifers Association.

Prisoners sentenced to life are considered a stabilizing influence in many prisons. Men who have been there for decades, and expect to die there, gradually settle into acceptance. They don't want trouble. They don't cause trouble. Often, they reach out to younger inmates in an effort to steer them from harm's way.

During The Day of Responsibility prisoners come face to face with the reality of their actions. Lifers use the opportunity to show younger inmates – ones who will eventually return home– just how their behavior affects their families, their communities and their victims.

It's not an easy thing to walk into a prison, especially one as large and imposing as the gray fortress that is Huntingdon, built in 1889. Like most of us, Lynn's perceptions of prison had been formed on the screen, in movies such as "The Shawshank Redemption" and "Escape from Alcatraz." So Lynn experienced major anxiety that day as she was led through security. Heavy steel doors unlocked and locked, clanging horribly, as she passed through sections of the prison. As she walked down a narrow corridor, men stood with their fingers wrapped around the bars of their cells, staring out at the attractive woman, their thoughts known only to themselves.

Finally, she and her victim advocate, Kathy Buckley, were led to the front of a small room with no windows, no air conditioning, and a single humming fan. About three dozen inmates sat between them and the exit. On what was an extraordinarily warm day for May, the room was already drenched in the smell of strong coffee and sweaty men.

As inmates grabbed a snack and a coffee, Lynn headed for a coffee pot. Immediately, a guard stepped up and advised her not to drink that coffee. He left the room and returned with a cup of coffee that he considered free of any "unidentifiable additions."

It was Lynn's first lesson about life behind bars.

Lesson two also came as a result of the coffee.

"When I accepted the coffee," Lynn said, "I certainly wasn't thinking ahead, as in where was the closest ladies room? Later I discovered a tiny bathroom in the back of the room that we all shared for the next several hours. I couldn't help but think, 'What have I gotten myself into?'"

Despite the grim reminders of where she was, Lynn was surprised by the inmates themselves. She was taken aback by their respect. Many stopped to say, "I'm sorry for your loss." "Thank you for sharing your story." "I don't think I would have the courage to do what you are doing."

They didn't match the ugly image Lynn had conjured up in her mind. "As I interacted with them, many of my preconceived notions disappeared that day," Lynn said. "Many of these individuals looked like people I encounter every day in my life. Some were young enough to be my children. They were serving time for their crimes, from drug possession to murder. Obviously, they needed to be here because they had made some really poor decisions and, in some cases, committed heinous acts, but it didn't make them horrible human beings. Each of them has the opportunity to learn from his mistakes, move forward and begin to make better choices. That applies even if they never leave prison as a result of the harm they caused."

Lynn wanted above all to reach the men. She wanted them to feel her pain and to understand the impact of crime. She hoped that her horrifying story would encourage these men to make positive changes in their attitudes and behaviors and instill in them the belief they could be instruments for change in their communities. She wanted each one to step up and become a better person, father, son, brother, mentor or friend.

The room was eerily quiet as she shared her story and pictures of Jen and Dave. She watched as several inmates pulled their tee shirts up to their faces as if to wipe sweat off their foreheads. Although they stared at the floor, they would occasionally look up. Only then could Lynn see it was not sweat, but tears, they were wiping away. Whether the tears were for the loss of Jen and Dave, the harm they had caused others or for themselves, Lynn would never know. But she hoped then, and she hopes today, that the tears were an acknowledgement of harm and a step towards being a better person.

When Lynn finished sharing her story, she opened the floor to questions. The inmates asked what happens to the money they pay to Pennsylvania's victim's compensation fund, which collects $35 for each felony and misdemeanor conviction and $25 from juvenile offenders. Lynn explained that the fund reimburses victims for expenses they incur as a result of a crime. The fund paid for her children's funeral, bought a marker for their grave and covered the cost of her counseling. As many inmates nodded, one said simply, "I will never again complain about those deductions."

When Lynn spoke of her children, she agonized over all she had missed. She never had a chance to see Dave drive for the first time or Jen walk down the aisle in her wedding gown. She told the inmates that every time she sees a baby, she imagines what it would have been like to be a grandmother.

Despite her great loss, Lynn injected humor into her talk. She told the inmates, "I even dream about David turning 40 and I would have to have that all-important talk with him, letting him know that maybe it would be a good idea to start to think about finding a place of his own." The inmates, startled by her humor, hesitated, but eventually the entire group laughed.

"A lifer talked with me afterwards and told me he has the same thoughts about his children," Lynn said. "He went on to say that his children visit him only a few times a year. I looked at him and told him I would trade places with him in a heartbeat. It was an odd encounter in an odd setting, but he understood. He apologized for being so insensitive."

In the years since that trip to Huntingdon, Lynn has taken her message to other inmates in other prisons. "Sometimes," she said, "the inmates will try to joke with me. One time an inmate motioned me over to him with his finger. I went over and he offered me a little advice: 'It's not a good idea to pick any fights while you're in here,' he said. I rolled my eyes and thanked him. Humor is good for everyone's soul."

"Inmates are curious," Lynn said. "The dialogue is more than just about my story; I give them an opportunity to ask me tough questions. I have fielded such questions as do I have other children? Will I have more children? Did I ever think about suicide? Do I believe in God? Did I forgive? Do I think 'they' are evil people? Do I believe in the death penalty? There is certainly more than just the death of Jen and Dave, and I am open to helping inmates further explore the far-reaching impact crime has over the course of a lifetime. I answer what I am comfortable with, and my answers have changed over the years."

While Lynn cannot be certain if all the inmates are sincere, she believes she reaches at least some of them. In a letter written from Huntingdon Prison, an inmate described how Lynn's words affected him. He was a batterer, an abusive man, serving time for his deeds.

He wrote:

> To the desk of
> Ms. Lynn Shiner
>
> I wish to relay my personal thanks to you first as a human being, and second as a man who has had two (Protection from Abuse) orders lodged against him. For the past several weeks I've been in a Batterers Prevention Group, not quite able to understand the full impact of my past actions. Ignorance defined "is simply not knowing." I can no longer claim ignorance, as a result of our encounter. While you spoke I had several epiphanies, and among these I've realized what a coward I've been, and just how selfish I was. I know now that abuse comes in many different forms and is a result of the perpetrator's own internalized shame, fears, anger, and diminished self-esteem issues. My time here at Huntingdon has been a long overdue awakening into my various character flaws and I've been proactive in making some

improvements in my ways of thinking by means of programs and self-help literature. Ms. Shiner ... I've been incarcerated all my life (state of mind); this prison is just a place. I've been a "Human Doing" not a "Human Being." The real tragedy is many won't realize nor accept this reality during the course of their lives. I don't want to die leaving my current circumstances as my legacy. It is my personal pledge and responsibility to try and prevent anyone from taking my path. I can no longer give excuses or complain because I don't know what tough is... You Do.

Sincerely,
(An inmate)

Before that first visit to a prison, Lynn worked with Kathy, her victim advocate, who not only prepared her for what was to come, but went with her into the prison and debriefed her afterwards. Because her ex-husband killed himself after murdering their children, Lynn had only marginal knowledge about the prison system. "I asked many of the same questions that I now know other victims ask," she said. "What do they do all day? Do they have TV, cable, phones? Are they really able to get college educations? What are they doing to help themselves? Are the programs mandatory? Are they allowed to write to their victims? Do they really have conjugal visits? What happens if they don't follow through with their programs? Can lifers ever get out? Are sex offenders housed with the general population?

"Kathy answered every question, and then took the time to walk me through exactly what my 'prison experience' would be like. From security, what I could and couldn't take in with me, what I should wear, why inmates wear different color uniforms, why some have brown shoes versus sneakers and more. She simply did everything possible that would allow me to walk in there with as much knowledge as possible. Afterwards, we discussed all aspects of the day, questions and comments the inmates shared. She validated my feelings and simply listened to my experience and answered more questions. I can't express how important an advocate is in working with inmates."

Six years after that first trip to Huntingdon, on a chilly February morning, I met Lynn, chipper as always, at the State Correctional Institution at Camp Hill, for what would be her 10th visit to a Pennsylvania prison. Lynn looked put together, professional, physically fit and brimming with confidence. Only someone who knows her well would understand that in this moment it was a façade. She was nervous, uncertain. She wanted the day to run perfectly. She wanted to say all the right things. By now, she would have gone over her speech a thousand times, changing a word here and there.

Nineteen years after the murders of her children, telling her story hasn't gotten any easier for Lynn. This day she relived the shocking details to 150 inmates facing her on folding chairs. They had asked to attend the session. Some find understanding in the words they hear. But prison officials admit that for others, the event simply offered a break from routine and an opportunity to feast on lunch and snacks beyond what's traditionally offered in the food lines.

Lynn always remains hopeful that she can be a catalyst for change. She answered inmates' questions, talked with them afterwards and participated in group discussions on forgiveness and repentance.

A week later Lynn received the following letter written by an inmate to his counselor:

> I spoke with you and told you how much Ms. Lynn's story moved me. Little did I know it would touch me even more once I returned to my cell and meditated upon her words. I cried as I replayed her every word, expression and non-verbal! I really wanted her to know how she helped me and empowered me to change. Please relay these words to her:

Dear Ms. Lynn,

Ever since you spoke yesterday my soul would not allow me any rest until I wrote you this letter. Over the past seven years, I've taken many programs but none has affected me like 'A Day of Responsibility.' Your story cut with precision through 31 years of pain and has started a process in me unlike any other program I've taken has.

Let me explain. My dad 'attempted' murder, suicide in our family when I was 14 years old. He took his life in front of me as I watched. I say attempted because my mom, as tenacious as she is, refused to die after he shot her. It has been 31 years since his death. Several things you said moved me to tears in my cell that night. I'll elaborate on a few. You said that you were not able to cry (in the moment you learned of Jen and Dave's murders). This hit me hard because for years I felt guilty for not being able to cry at my dad's funeral. But it was what you "didn't say" that spoke the loudest to me. Behind your voice I could still see and hear a love and determination for your precious children and an ideal of what should have been had it not been for the selfish act of an individual.

Ms. Lynn that is what inspired me to want to be an even better man. I no longer will be the cause of pain in any way, shape or form for anything or anyone.

I realized through your pain, that it was the pain that I disassociated myself from all these years. Let me try to explain Ms. Lynn. I have been hurting others through crimes and relationships all these years and then I would disassociate myself from the pain and take no responsibility. What I have been doing is reliving my traumatic experience over and over again, inflicting my unresolved pain on others. That's by no means an excuse but just an observation that I made through your honesty. So thank you for sharing your pain, because through it I was able to see deeper in my own life than I ever have. Thank you for sharing your sorrow because through it, I was finally able to cry.

Please never stop telling your story and allowing the voices of your precious babies to speak into the lives of men and women like me.

Sincerely,
(An inmate)

Maybe Lynn saved a life that day. She will never know. Her fervent hope is that if she can change just one person, there might be one less victim. But the work takes its toll. Sharing her story, reliving the horror, wears her down. She returns home exhausted, yet filled with a sense of peace and accomplishment.

Lynn's journey has included many new and unusual experiences, but everything she does is meant to honor Jen and Dave. Some of her rewards and efforts include the following:

In 1995-96, Lynn received the Service to Mankind award from the local Sertoma Club. The presenter said, "The person chosen not only made a difference in the lives of others but has overcome great personal tragedy to make such a difference by selflessly dedicating her life to help victims of crime. Despite living with horrible emotional pain, she works diligently to spare others from having to go through what she has had to endure. Her courage and strength in helping others have become the hallmarks of her life and an inspiration to all who know her."

In 1997, Lynn and her friend Ruth Brown organized the first Y Walk or Run 5K. Lynn was an active committee member and subcommittee chairwoman for the Y Walk Against Violence. With the help of many, the community awareness event raised more than $20,000 for the YWCA's Domestic Violence and Rape Crisis departments.

In the mid to late 1990s, "Lost Dreams on Canvas" was shown in the Rotunda of the U.S. Senate and in the Pennsylvania Capitol. An anti-violence art project, formerly housed at the Pennsylvania Academy of the Fine Arts, the show included Jen and Dave's portraits. Theirs is one of nearly 400 portraits painted by volunteer artists to memorialize the lives of young victims of violence in hopes of ending this plague.

In 2000, Lynn was featured in the book, "Transcending, Reflections of Crime Victims" by Howard Zehr. The book includes portraits and stories of 39 courageous victims of violent crime. His hope was "that this book might hand down a rope to others who have experienced such tragedies and traumas, and that it might allow all who read it to live on the healing edge."

Several years later, Ingrid De Sanctis, a writer and director, asked to include Lynn's story in "Transcending" in a play described as "a living, kinetic portrait of crime victims." The play, "A Body in Motion," presents the challenges and triumphs of individuals who are coping with violence and moving through that violence to a place of transcendence while reminding the audience that these are our neighbors, our friends and sometimes ourselves. The intention is to remind the audience of "the strength of the human spirit and the fragility of life."

In 2004, with the support of the Pennsylvania Commission on Crime and Delinquency, the Pennsylvania Department of Corrections, the Prison Society and the Office of the Victim Advocate, "A Body in Motion" traveled across the state and was performed in eight state prisons for inmates during the day and in communities at night. The play also was performed in other statewide and national venues.

Lynn said, "No matter how many times I watched this play, it overwhelmed me, and each time I would sob uncontrollably. I also formed an instant bond with Allison and Trent, the actors who played Jen and Dave. I can't tell you how much it meant to me that they came right up to me after the very first viewing and gave me the biggest hug. Allison and I stood there and cried.

"Probably the most memorable viewing was in Graterford prison. I decided to watch the play with the inmates. Without a doubt, the words and actions had an impact. After the play the inmates were given the opportunity to ask questions, and one inmate asked a question about the portion of the play that related to Jen and Dave. He was visibly upset and couldn't understand how a father could do that to his own child. He asked several questions about the mother. The actors were ready to answer, but they stopped as I stood up and slowly turned to face 500 inmates and introduced myself as Jen and Dave's mother. You could have heard a pin drop. I proceeded to answer their questions. In that moment, I was broken and exhausted from watching the play, but I wanted each of them to know how real it was and is."

On April 22, 2004, during National Crime Victims' Rights Week, Attorney General John Ashcroft presented Lynn with the National Crime Victims' Service Award for her work with the Jen and Dave Law and with overhauling Pennsylvania's Victims Compensation Assistance Program.

The award is given annually by the attorney general and the president to honor extraordinary individuals and programs that provide services to victims of crime and exemplify the long-term commitment that characterizes many of our nation's victim service providers, some of whom are also victims of crime.

Lynn was able to take Paul and her parents with her for the two-day event. Lynn said, "My parents could not have been prouder. They told everyone, especially my Mom. I thought she had told everyone, until we arrived at McDonald's for a quick breakfast on our way to D.C., where she shared the news with the workers behind the counter. We drove so far and then took the train into D.C. There was my Mom telling the people in the train sitting next to us about her daughter. They didn't speak or understand English. Even the taxi driver heard about me.

"The evening before the ceremony, we were treated to a night of entertainment and several speakers. I can recall my Mom complaining to the U.S. assistant attorney general about not being able to hear her when she spoke, and she apologized to my mother. The day of the event, the assistant attorney general stood before an audience of 500-plus people and opened the ceremony with 'Mrs. Monk, can you hear me now?'

"It was a beautiful ceremony that was attended by family members, friends and co-workers."

In 2004, Lynn received the Edith Surgan Award from the National Organization of Victim Assistance. The award is given to a victim or survivor who demonstrates a life of commitment to promote rights and services to help change the lives of victims.

Lynn is especially proud of the new initiatives and changes that have come under her leadership at the Pennsylvania Commission on Crime and Delinquency. Among them are the following:

In 2002, Lynn was instrumental in making significant changes to Pennsylvania's Crime Victims Act, especially in the areas of crime victim compensation eligibility and payments. Since its creation in 1995, the Victims' Services Advisory Committee (VSAC) has set a priority on revamping victims' compensation policies, procedures, rules and regulations, and law in order to create a victim-centered program that is inclusive and beneficial to as many crime victims in Pennsylvania as is feasible and financially possible.

In 2007, the Survivor's Speakers Bureau created opportunities to empower survivors who are far enough along in their journey to talk about their experiences to community groups and organizations. There is no greater messenger to speak of impact than a crime victim.

Once a survivor has successfully completed the training, opportunities are made available to them, such as training, legislative hearings, victim impact panels, victims' rights rallies and media interviews to share their experiences and help strengthen how services are delivered across Pennsylvania.

In 2008, PA SAVIN (Pennsylvania's Statewide Automated Victim Information & Notification) system was rolled out. SAVIN provides automated notifications to victims when an offender in a county jail, state prison or under state parole supervision within the commonwealth is released, transferred, or escapes.

PA SAVIN is a free service that broadens the reach of notification, as anyone can register, such as family members and friends of the crime victim. Law enforcement officers and court officials can use the system to track repeat offenders, and concerned citizens can keep posted on the incarceration status of an inmate who committed a crime in their neighborhood.

In 2010, the Pennsylvania Crime Victims website was launched, www.pacrimevictims.com, to help those whose lives have been forever changed by violence and crime. The primary focus is to let crime victims know they are not alone and that help is available. The website, the first of its kind in the country, provides information on trauma and healing, how to follow an offender through the criminal and juvenile justice system, rights and services available to crime victims statewide and in specific counties and how to obtain financial help and free counseling. Crime victims also can learn how to sign up for notification when perpetrators are released from prison.

In 2012, the Data Collection, Reporting and Outcomes Project (DCROP) launched. It is a collaborative initiative among state funders that aims to provide all state-funded victim service programs a streamlined, standardized data system that reduces the administrative burden, allowing more time to focus on the needs of crime victims.

In 2011, Lynn was appointed director of the Office of Victims' Services. In this position, she is involved in the strategic planning and development of an integrated plan to effectively meet the needs of crime victims throughout Pennsylvania through the distribution of more than $30 million dollars in state and federal funding. Lynn also provides oversight of the Victims Compensation Assistance Program.

Lynn will have provided 35 years of service to the Commonwealth of Pennsylvania in January of 2014. She looks forward to the next phase of her journey, which will always involve being a voice for victims of crime.

Chapter 12

Nancy's New Path

Nancy suffered from a bit of empty-nest syndrome when Randi married Brian in 2000. For the first time in her life, she was alone and could focus on her own needs. But Randi was close by, and she was always able to keep their connection intact.

That changed with Randi's murder.

"I spent 15 years of my life going to college at night," Nancy said. "My goal was to finish my master's when I turned 40. After obtaining my master's, I needed to find my own outlet and allow Randi and Brian to enjoy their life together. I had discussions with my advisor from Penn State about going to law school. His advice was to spend my money on dance lessons, since I had an established career in state government.

"Well, that dream of going back to college was washed away when Randi died. Perhaps what happened on May 4, 2012, has fulfilled my dream now. I was given an honorary doctorate from Central Penn College for my work as a community advocate for the rights of domestic violence victims. Receiving that honor told me that my work in the community is where I should be."

Greg said Nancy quickly became energized. "It didn't take long after Randi was murdered for her to realize she had to do something to see this doesn't happen to anyone else," he said.

Nancy channeled her energy into fighting domestic violence. The cause seemed appropriate given Brian's involvement in Randi's death and Nancy's history.

Nancy had been a college freshman when she met Randi's father. Gary was stationed with the Navy in Virginia, and seemed worldly to the shy girl from a tight-knit family in Mechanicsburg, Pa.

At the end of her first semester, Gary asked Nancy's parents for her hand in marriage. The young couple planned to marry in two years when his tour ended.

The proposal went badly. Nancy's father, the son of immigrants, put great stock in education. Nancy would be the family's first college graduate. Marriage, he feared, would impede that goal.

Her mother was more concerned about her naiveness. "No, no," she said. "This is not going to happen. You are too young and don't know what you are getting yourself into. You have only known this man for months. What do you know about love?"

As Nancy learned, mothers often know best.

Since she was still living at home, her parents thought they could keep Nancy from Gary. They forbid her to see him. They monitored her calls. They didn't anticipate her determination to be with the man she loved. Gary had said he loved Nancy. She had lost her virginity to him. To Nancy, that meant they should be together.

In January 1974, three days after Nancy's 19th birthday, she loaded her belongings into Gary's car, went with him to a justice of the peace, and said, "I do." Then she headed off with him in the rain to Norfolk, where he was stationed.

Nancy cried most of the way. She had deceived her parents. She felt lonely. She secretly hoped her father would pull up alongside them and demand she go home. Instead, she found herself in Norfolk in a one-bedroom apartment filled with old furniture and new rules, Gary's rules. Gary was the boss, and he had expectations. He wanted the apartment clean, his uniforms washed, starched and ironed. He wanted dinner on the table when he arrived home. Sometimes he brought friends to dinner and sat and drank with them all evening. This prompted another rule: No bitching, especially in front of his friends.

Nancy went from Gary's princess to being cursed at, chastised and belittled. He threw things and shoved her when he wanted her attention. One day, he slapped her, beginning the pattern of abuse. Gary would hit or punch or kick. Then he would apologize and promise it would never happen again. A promise that he didn't keep.

In the spring, Nancy discovered she was pregnant. Lonely and scared, she called her parents on April 16, her mother's birthday. The news of a grandchild due at Christmas brought reconciliation. Soon there were weekend visits home and a baby shower.

Gary was the excited, expectant father in front of others. At home, he was a ticking time bomb. Nancy was seven months pregnant the night of her worst beating. Gary kicked her, dragged her to the sidewalk and punched her in the face. She lost consciousness.

He said it was her fault.

She learned to cover her bruises with makeup and dream up excuses for any oddities in his behavior. Nancy didn't want anyone to know of the trouble in paradise. She wanted people to think they were happy and very much in love.

Randi Lee was born at 3 p.m. on a Sunday, weighing 8 pounds, 10 ounces. From the start, she loved being the center of attention. The first grandchild, she delighted Nancy's parents, who would babysit, buy her clothes and take her to Hills department store for $1 baby pictures. Her first picture shows her at three months, holding herself up and posing, like a beauty in a swimsuit contest.

Randi was five before Nancy found the strength to leave her marriage. By then, her husband had left the Navy and the family had moved back to Pennsylvania. Several times, he changed jobs to advance his career, and they changed residences – never too close to her family. Wherever they lived, Nancy always lived in fear, bound by Gary's rules. When he was unhappy, Nancy paid for it.

When she finally left him, she put her belongings in storage, moved in with her sister and landed an entry-level job with the state. She began taking courses, one per semester, at Harrisburg Area Community College.

Everything she did was for Randi. Randi was always under her wing and not allowed to be with anyone Nancy didn't know. When Nancy went to class, her family watched Randi.

Most of the time, it was Randi and Nancy. They would sled, ice skate, roller skate, ride bikes, swim and do all sorts of activities together. Where Randi went, Nancy went too. They were mother and daughter, but sometimes they seemed more like best friends. It was a line that blurred more and more as Randi became a young woman.

After the horrifying loss of her daughter and best friend, Nancy sat at her kitchen table in 2005 with her friend Deborah Donahue, former executive director of Domestic Violence Services of Cumberland & Perry Counties, and in just eight weeks they organized the first Randi's Race: A 5K/ Walk and Run for Hope and Courage. In its first nine years, Randi's Race raised more than $270,000 to support Randi's House of Angels and the Domestic Violence Services of Cumberland & Perry Counties.

"The most rewarding part of my life is to be able to do something for someone else," Nancy said.

That isn't to say that Nancy doesn't still suffer from her loss. "I have my crazy moments, my sad moments, my depressing moments, but I'm lucky that I still have the opportunity to talk about whatever is on my mind. It has been interesting, as time passed, how my comfort level got easier for me. I could finally admit that I had been abused, and I could discuss Randi's death openly."

The woman who had been ashamed of her abuse, who had hidden it from her family and friends, was gone. Taking her place was a determined mother who wanted women and men to open their eyes and see the abuse around them and to focus on how it impacts children.

"Since 2004," Nancy said, "I have spoken before many groups about how I am a victim of domestic violence twice in my life now. I talk openly about the abuse that I endured as a young bride and Randi's murder. The venues of my audiences include students in college, educators, community groups, businesses and state agencies, such as the Pennsylvania Board of Probation and Parole and the Department of Corrections. I have talked to staff who educate and work with prisoners, juveniles in detention centers and students. I have attended the Cumberland County Victims' Rights Rally candlelight vigils since 2004, and the Shippensburg University Victim Impact Classes. I was the keynote speaker for Crime Victims' Rights Week in 2011 at the State Capitol and at the Pennsylvania Commission on Crime and Delinquency's, Office of Victims' Services, Pathways conference.

"I have been honored to speak before larger groups address-ing issues that impact victims. The Pennsylvania Newspaper Association invited me to sit on a panel and talk about the sensitivity of media to crime victims, where the audience consisted of reporters and the questions were geared toward how media could improve its coverage of crime. In 2011, I was invited to speak before the Pennsylvania Association of Broadcasters about media and victimization."

All of this was strange territory for a woman who grew up in a family where the best thing you could do was live your life quietly and not draw attention to yourself.

"A lot of people ask how I have the guts to speak in front of others," Nancy said. "How do I prepare for it? What motivates me? I always had a comfort level for talking in front of others. My profession required me to present to advisory boards and people in leadership positions. This helped me to overcome any phobias.

"I have a comfort level now when I speak before audiences that want to hear about me or Randi. I know that they are sincere and will give me their undivided attention. I know that some will walk away with a lesson learned and others will always shed tears before I finish my story."

Nancy never speaks on a whim. She's organized and prepared. She takes public speaking seriously and spends hours in preparation.

"How do I do it? I simply speak from my heart. I have lived through two tragedies that have given me lessons learned for a century. I spend a lot of time preparing. It is a process. I start by formulating my thoughts as I exercise or take a shower. I put an outline together and build from it day after day. I seek out thoughts and opinions from my support group and begin to write. I rehearse for hours. The last two days I rehearse over and over in front of the mirror, making sure that I do not read directly from my notes. No matter how many times I tell my story, I shed tears.

"I remember giving a speech at the victims' rally. I could not help but cry when I told the audience about my unconditional love for Randi. I apologized to everyone. A man came up to me and told me that seeing me cry showed him how much I loved Randi.

"The night before any speaking engagement, I pray to Randi that she will be by my side. Right before I walk up to the podium, I take three deep breaths and close my eyes, remembering Randi the last time I saw her."

Although she has worked hard at perfecting her public speaking skills, Nancy encountered one group that made her extremely uncomfortable.

Nancy met Lynn in 2006 when she took a job at the Pennsylvania Commission on Crime and Delinquency, where Lynn worked.

"I can remember how scared I was to meet her," Nancy said. "I did not know what to say to another mother who had lost her children. Everyone in the agency had so much respect for all that she had done for crime victims. It took me about four months to actually walk down to the second floor and introduce myself. I rehearsed what I would say with hope that I would not disrespect her. I hoped that she could relate to where I was in my life."

They quickly bonded, in part because they could sense each other's pain. Two years later, Lynn took Nancy with her to the Huntingdon State Correctional Institution, where she talked to inmates about the impact of crime. Inside the large stone penitentiary, Nancy sat in awe. "It was very comforting to me, the way she just took control of the audience." Still, Nancy couldn't shake her unease. Her daughter's killers are inmates in similar prisons. Realistically, she knew they weren't in the audience. Emotionally, she was a wreck. "I just couldn't look at the prisoners. I just didn't want to touch their hands or anything," she said. "It was really tough for me."

Still, Nancy remained determined to face other audiences. In February 2007, she joined the first class of the Survivors Speakers Bureau sponsored by the Pennsylvania Commission on Crime and Delinquency. It was the first time she had encountered other crime victims, all of whom were training to share their stories as part of a mission to make others understand what crime does to victims.

"I was so taken back to think that so many people are impacted by other crimes, and not just homicide. I met sisters, mothers, fathers that told of how a crime impacted their lives. I learned how to deliver my message and how I could be a resource to others. I shared my emotions with them and also saw how crime can destroy a person. Just being in their presence showed me that I was not alone. How I coped with Randi's loss was not uncommon; there were others coping with their trauma and recovery. I remain a member of the Survivors Speakers Bureau. My focus now is to learn more about political advocacy and how I can be a resource to changing legislation."

It seemed that Nancy was on a path to learning more about herself. In particular, she would learn just how strong she could be.

"In 2006, while attending the Pennsylvania Conference for Women, so many women thanked me and made me proud to be chosen to be honored among 50 Women in Pennsylvania at the event.

At the same time, the Pennsylvania Commission for Women Role Model book, "Voices," was being launched and there was one woman who had read my story. She said how touched she was by my story and told me that I was a 'woman of courage and resiliency.' Resiliency? What did that mean? So I went home and looked up that word."

The dictionary defined it as "the power or ability to return to the original form, position, etc., after being bent, compressed, or stretched; elasticity or the ability to recover readily from illness, depression, adversity, or the like; buoyancy."

So there it was. Nancy was resilient. Others saw her that way.

"It was a new beginning for me," she said. "How I was seen by others with high expectations. It was time for me to recognize that I had no other obligations that would stop me. I had no other children and was not married.

"Perhaps my resiliency helped me to move forward, reconnect with my family, create a new life for myself and bounce back to who I once was. It helped me to set goals to help other victims of crime.

"My challenge was to avoid negative thoughts and emotions that I faced each day, whether it was dealing with four years of the appellate court (for an appeal filed by Brian Trimble) or fighting NBC's 'Dateline' to prevent it from showing a crime scene photo.

"I live each day avoiding negative people and situations that create stress for me. I focus my efforts on replacing those negative emotions with positive thinking, creating new ideas, expressing creativity. I see myself as a change agent."

Some of that change involved the media.

After Nancy's disappointment with "Dateline" and the photos of Randi that had been aired, she went to New York to meet the executive producer. She was accompanied by Judy Yupcavage, who was then director of communications for the Pennsylvania Coalition Against Domestic Violence, Deb Donahue, then director of the Domestic Violence Services of Cumberland & Perry Counties; and Donna VandeMortel, then director of Cumberland County Victim Services Division. After a disappointing meeting, they returned, and Nancy formed the Dissemination and Access of Crime Scene Photos Task Force under the direction and support of the Pennsylvania Coalition Against Domestic Violence, the Office of the Victim Advocate, the Pennsylvania Commission on Crime and Delinquency, and the Cumberland County Victim Services Division.

Its aim was to ensure that victims of crime and their families are treated with dignity, respect and sensitivity in the dissemination of graphic crime scene images. It included individuals from state justice agencies, county justice agencies, victims' advocates, the media and others.

The task force researched how the Constitution protects our right to free speech and policies that prohibit sharing crime scene photos. The task force determined that when graphic crime scene images are disseminated without the knowledge and/or consent of victims for the sole purpose of sensationalism and/or profit, they enhance the trauma and long-lasting effects to victims and their families.

Nancy also launched an effort to prevent violent acts perpetuated by video games. "I had learned as part of the investigation that Brian had spent numerous hours playing 'Dungeons and Dragons' and other role-playing games," Nancy said. "His connection to Blaine Norris heightened his desire to play video games at home and at work.

"In my research to advocate against violent video games, I was introduced to Professor Fred Arensmeyer of the Widener University School of Law. As part of a research project, law students examined the website Hitman.com that Brian used to learn how to kill a person.

"Unfortunately, the research project provided insight into how the website has no place of origin and how impossible it is to have a website removed from a public domain."

Early in Nancy's journey, she went with her mother to a support group at her mother's church. "She had found out about this group from a friend who had lost her daughter in Iraq. It was ironic that her friend's daughter had graduated with Randi from Trinity High School.

"Each week we visited different homes. Each week I heard their stories. I always knew that my mother meant well, but I would notice how much of a toll it took on her. There would be 10 or 15 people telling us about their loss. I got so emotionally drained that I had to stop going."

Not to be deterred, Nancy founded her own support group in 2006. Restoring our Souls is a support group for victims of domestic violence homicide in Cumberland and Perry counties. Members include surviving family members and close friends of victims, and the group is committed to helping them cope with their tragedy and the grieving process. Members of the group also serve as a resource to the Cumberland County district attorney's office in developing protocol for responding to the needs of crime victims.

Nancy has kept busy with many other groups and events. When the Harrisburg Bar Association sponsored a session on victimization as it related to homicide, she served on a panel with the Cumberland and Adams county district attorneys. "The audience," she said, "was interested in hearing from a survivor, the pros and cons on how the criminal justice system treated me, and what information was shared with me."

In 2011, Governor Ed Rendell and the Pennsylvania Commission on Crime and Delinquency hosted representatives from a Russian criminal justice department. Nancy was invited to join Cumberland County Court of Common Pleas Judge Skip Ebert in providing the details of Randi's case. She spoke about the criminal justice system from the victims' perspective, assistance from the Victim Advocates office, and her experience with the death penalty.

In 2012 she served as a member of the Restitution in Pennsylvania Task Force. Its job was to make recommendations to significantly improve state laws and procedures related to the quality of restitution ordering, collection and disbursement to crime victims.

The 39-member task force, chaired by the governor's Victim Advocate, was comprised of representatives from all three branches of state government, counties, the criminal and juvenile justice systems, advocacy groups and crime victims. Over a 12-month period, they were to determine how to maximize the reimbursement of financial losses to crime victims. The recommendations of the task force included the establishment of restitution funds and programs throughout both the criminal and juvenile justice systems, placing defendants on a single electronic payment plan to ensure that prior, older cases are not neglected in favor of the most current case, and legislation to authorize courts to order wage attachment for defendants who have been found in contempt for nonpayment of restitution, costs or fines.

Nancy was selected in 2010 as the first recipient of the "Thanks to You" Community Hero Award from Central Pennsylvania Dunkin' Donuts.

In 2011 she received the first Annual 2012 Direct Energy and Patriot News Harrisburg Volunteer Citizen of the Year Award for her advocacy and for helping women in crisis.

Despite her awards and her participation on panels and task forces, Nancy's focus continues to be Randi's House of Angels, a place where children exposed to domestic violence can find safety and support.

Since its creation in October 2011, this tribute to Randi has established itself as a highly visible service agency working with agencies throughout central Pennsylvania. Its partners include the YWCA of Greater Harrisburg, Victim/Witness Assistance Program of Dauphin County, ACCESS-York and its Victim Assistance Center, Domestic Violence Intervention of Lebanon County Inc., and Domestic Violence Services of Cumberland & Perry Counties.

The services provided by Randi's House of Angels include therapy for children, as well as a three-day summer camp program for children 8-13 who have experienced domestic violence.

The first camps operated in 2010 and 2011. Through educational and interpersonal activities, campers focus on increasing their self-esteem and confidence. Randi's Camp aims to let children know they are valuable contributors to the family unit and that their thoughts are worthy of expression.

"For the longest time, I came home from work each day and just felt so useless," Nancy said. "Once I decided to move forward, it has been nonstop for me. Now, when I come home from work, I go directly to my laptop and work on all the administrative tasks related to her foundation. I am self-educating from research and training on how to build the capacity of a nonprofit. I know that this project has given me hope that I can make a difference. I know that one day I will tell others that I started RHOA from my kitchen table. One day I want others to say that I established a safe place for children of domestic violence."

It is Nancy's passion to continue the legacy of her daughter Randi through her efforts to advocate against domestic violence and help children. This is her fitting tribute to the memory of the daughter she loves and lost.

Chapter 13

The Ripple Effect

September 11, 2001

Many of us immediately recall it was a Tuesday morning when the first plane went into the Twin Towers. Most of us know exactly where we were.

As a nation, we went into shock. We were in a national state of disbelief. Why, we asked, would anyone do this to another human being? We couldn't make sense of what had occurred, but we began grieving along with those who were personally affected by the massive tragedy.

December 24, 2002

The Christmas Eve disappearance of Laci Peterson, a California woman who was seven months pregnant with her first child, had Americans glued to their television sets. Everyone seemed to have an opinion about where she was and whether she was alive.

Nancy and Randi were among those who watched as the media covered every aspect of the mystery of the missing woman. The news that her husband, Scott Peterson, was the primary suspect was horrifying. How could anyone harm a woman and her unborn child, especially the father of that child?

Laci was last seen alive only three weeks prior to Randi's murder.

That left Nancy watching alone as Laci's story unfolded, and she became obsessed with following every twist and turn. In many ways, it was like looking into a crystal ball as she considered the similarities between Laci and Randi and the men they had married.

From Nancy's vantage point, Scott Peterson and Brian had much in common. Like Scott Peterson, Brian had changed his appearance after Randi's murder and began living a lifestyle unfamiliar to Nancy. His actions and the changes in his personality mimicked Scott Peterson. Both husbands denied any wrongdoing. Both craved their freedom at any cost.

Both were convicted of first degree murder and are featured in a book written by Dr. Robi Ludwig, "'Till Death Do Us Part: Love, Marriage, and the Mind of the Killer Spouse."

December 14, 2012
Sandy Hook Elementary School

A shooter entered the Connecticut school at 9:35 a.m., 11 days before Christmas. In less than 20 minutes, 20 children were dead.

When she heard the news, Lynn immediately fixated on their last minutes, the dwindling seconds of those children's lives. What was going through their minds? She flashed back to David. What was he thinking as he struggled with his knife-wielding father?

When Lynn saw the footage of parents gathered outside the school, waiting as children were released several at a time, she couldn't imagine the relief experienced by those who saw a familiar face. Then, when school officials said no more children would be coming out, she began to feel a heaviness on her chest. She knew exactly what those parents were about to experience.

Lynn had reached her limit. Now she had to monitor how much more she could take in.

Crime is like a stone tossed into a pond. The initial impact begins with a splash, but the splash quickly becomes a ripple. Then the ripple slowly expands, farther and farther, until it impacts the entire pond.

When a crime occurs, the first major splash is the direct victim. Then comes a phone call in the night or police knocking on the door, bringing the impact to the immediate family. Soon the ripples reach out to close friends, extended family, neighbors, classmates, teachers, and co-workers. Their first thoughts are, "No, it can't be." Maybe they heard it wrong. Perhaps it's another person with the same name.

Before long, the ripples impact strangers. Neighbors no longer feel safe. They shut themselves in and lock their doors. From a single home to a street to an entire neighborhood or town, the impact of crime reverberates.

Crime can affect first responders as well as those who work in the criminal justice system. A detective who responded to the murder scene orchestrated by Tom Snead could no longer continue in his job. But he tucked a picture of Jen and Dave in his wallet and carried it with him, a lifelong reminder of how precious life is.

When Lynn visited her children's grave a year after their death, she found wrapped Christmas presents from their cousin Bob covering their marker. Tucked underneath the gifts was a business card left by a Lower Paxton Twp. police officer. His card served as a gesture of respect and a quiet reminder of the lasting impact of crime.

The individuals in this chapter all have been part of Nancy's and Lynn's journeys. They have reflected, in their own words, on the impact of the deaths of Randi, Jen and Dave. Many remember where they were and what they were doing a decade or two ago when the ripples from the crime reached them.

David Freed
District Attorney, Cumberland County, Pennsylvania

The night that Randi was murdered, my wife and I left our 1½-year-old son, Tommy, (now 10) with a babysitter and went out for dinner with my wife's parents. Our purpose was to inform them that we were expecting our second child (Elizabeth, who was born September 3, 2003). As our dinner was ending, I received a page and instructions to head to a crime scene on Wood Street, not far from my house in Camp Hill. My memory of that night will always be going from an occasion of great joy to an occasion of tragic sadness and waste. I have two lasting impressions from that night: the violence indicated in the garage where Randi's body lay – and the obvious attempt to make the house look like it was burglarized.

During the course of the investigation and leading up to the resolution of the case, I came to know Nancy Chavez. In the ensuing years, as I have told Nancy before, I often think of Randi when I look at my Elizabeth. I share a special bond with her because of Randi that I plan to explain to her when she is old enough to understand. My children -- we now have 3 -- know about Randi's Race and about domestic violence, but I want to make sure Elizabeth knows that she shares a connection to Randi and her family, just as I do. I have often said in my business I meet some of the best people in the worst of circumstances, and Randi's murder is a prime example.

Gregory Green
Nancy's Boyfriend

On the evening of December 24, 2002, I had the pleasure of sharing Christmas Eve dinner with Nancy, her mother, her sister and brother-in-law, Linda and Mike, their son, Michael Joseph, and Randi and Brian. It was my first time meeting everyone, except Nancy, Randi, and Brian. I was nervous, but so grateful that I had been invited to share a very special occasion with a wonderful family.

Less than three weeks later, I received a phone call from Nancy's brother-in-law, Mike, informing me that Randi had been found murdered in her garage. It was and still is one of the saddest days of my life. I cried and I swore. I just couldn't believe that God would let this happen to Randi.

Months later, when it started to become apparent that Brian was involved with Randi's murder, it made me realize that sometimes we really don't know the "other" side of people. Brian was a Jekyll and Hyde. I thought he was this loving, vulnerable guy with MS. He was and is an evil, manipulative coward.

Gabriella Camplese
Randi's Best Friend

I was lucky enough to know Randi and her family for close to 14 years. Randi and I met in high school. We became close friends, racked up countless phone minutes, kept in touch throughout college, vacationed together, supported each other through difficult times, and helped plan each other's weddings. We laughed, cried, and laughed some more... One thing we always did was have fun.

Randi was my friend for 14 years. She always supported me, worried about me, and stood by me whatever my decisions were, whether she agreed with them or not. There are not many people I can say that about. Randi not only touched my life through the years, but the lives of so many others through her own relationship with them, her relationship with her mother, and her hard work and dedication to her profession.

I am lucky to have had the chance to know such a beautiful woman, who brought so much happiness and inspiration to all of us and everything that she encountered. There was one common theme, Randi's smile, her laugh, her love for life. I only hope that through our memories of Randi and how she touched our lives that we realize the effect our words and our actions have on people...

A line from one of the letters that I received from a dear college friend of Randi's struck me. "Perhaps the greatest gift you gave me is the memory of you."

Steve Marquart
Randi's Best Friend

Randi was taken away from my life at a time when I was still finding who I was. Her life and tragic death were truly formative influences in my life and who I am today. Randi was a very good friend who instilled positive relationships and people values through her example. From her I learned how to open up and be more social. To this day, I value the relationships she built and have used them as a guide to create my own friendships. Although her death was a tragic experience, the goodness she left behind will always prevail. Randi was the glue that kept our group of lifelong friends together, and in her death those special friendships continue. Randi and her spirit continue to bless those of us who call her friend.

Heidi Klimpke
Randi's Colleague from Penn State Hershey Medical Center

Having met Randi at work, we spent a great deal of time together chatting about friends, family, plans, and just plain life. I quickly grew to know her as a tireless worker, obsessive planner, deeply devoted daughter, and true blue friend. I was expecting my first child and Randi talked endlessly of how she, too, couldn't wait to be a mother. She planned for the day when she thought she might be the caregiver to her husband, due to a debilitating disease.

She was the light of her mother's life and put family first in everything she did.

I now pass the cemetery where my friend, my coworker, is buried. Buried along with her dreams for the future. Randi's death shook me to my core. It was a realization that unknown evil is among us and bad things happen to good people. People that I know. I think of all that was taken away by one insane selfish act, and to this day I am filled with a profound sadness. I no longer see the best in people but now have a mistrust of all.

I no longer watch the news or read newspaper articles about violent acts. I do not watch movies or TV shows with crime-ridden stories of murder. Randi wasn't just another story. She was a bright shining star whose light was darkened too early by the devious acts of cowards.

Jill Berry
Randi's Childhood Best Friend

I think the biggest way Randi's murder impacted my life is that I lost one of my very best friends. I miss not being able to grow older with her, raise our children together, and create more lifelong memories together. Sadly, I don't trust people like I used to. Brian made it hard to do that. I counted him as a friend, too, and when someone you trust does something so unspeakable, it really makes you think twice about how well you know others.

Linda Wilson
Nancy's Sister and Randi's Aunt

As a young girl, Randi was the little sister I never had. She was part of our nuclear family, like the fifth girl. She was dearly loved by my mother and father and was the first grandchild in our family. Our family watched as Randi blossomed into a responsible young lady, starting a career and new marriage.

Life could not be better until the cold, rainy night on January 10, 2003, which put an end to all of Randi's dreams. When I think of that night, a deep sadness fills my heart. I can visualize her entering her house, thinking about her husband and how they would spend the night together by their Christmas tree, which was still standing from the holidays. Her innocent thoughts filled her head while her murderer was getting ready to pounce upon her like a lion upon his prey. I can see this beast hurting my dear niece, and there was no one to help her. She struggled, suffered, and died alone.

This is what hurts the most, and my eyes fill with tears writing this. There was always someone there to help Randi while she was growing up -- mom, dad, Nancy, my sisters, Mike and me -- and none of us was there to save her.

Michael Wilson
Randi's Cousin

At the time of Randi's death, I was only eight years old. My mother was pregnant with my little sister, Isabela. I do not remember much about that day when my parents found out about my cousin's death. I remember my father coming home and both of my parents being very distraught and confused, but most of all crying. I also remember my Nana, Aunt Rose, and Cousin Joey coming over to hear the news. It was truly a shock to everyone to hear of Randi's death. I had just seen Randi at my Aunt Nancy's house over Christmas break.

Since I was only eight, I did not realize how horrific the details of the case were until my parents told me. Since I was so young at the time, my parents held the secrets of the case away from me. Today, I know that Randi is in a much better place now. Although her innocent life was taken away, I know that Randi is helping to fight against domestic violence every day in her spirit looking down on all of us as our guardian angel.

Brenda Gould
Randi's College Roommate and Associate at Penn State
Hershey Medical Center

Randi's death was a shock and a devastating loss for her family and friends. It was hard to deal with the senselessness of her death, and initially it was a scary time not knowing who did it or why they did it. Then it made me angry that someone whom Randi loved could just end her life with little remorse.

At the same time, it made you think of your own life, because it was a reminder of how short life can truly be. Randi lived life to the fullest, and that is where I take comfort. I can still see her smile when I think of her.

I am glad that her mom turned this tragedy into something positive by starting Randi's Race. It is a way to honor and remember a life well lived. I wish we didn't have to do this and that she was still here, but it makes it a little easier to know that we are helping others because of her. I think that exemplifies Randi's life, as she wanted to help people, which she did by being a speech therapist, a friend, and loving daughter.

It doesn't hurt as much to think of her as it did in that first year, and I'm glad I have fond memories of Randi.

Randi's Aunt Emily

When we lost Randi, there was sadness, anger, and why's. She was taken from us so suddenly in a senseless death. We had to learn to accept the loss and heal.

There were happy memories when Randi and her mother, Nancy, would come to Kansas to attend the family reunion. She was so happy visiting us. They left us such lovely memories.

Life can be thought of as a race in which everyone runs the short distance. For some, the race is over too soon. We are a large family, and talking about Randi and sharing her happy times helped the healing process. We keep her in our prayers and know that our dear Lord was there to welcome her home.

Lara Young
Randi's College Roommate

I have written this letter in my head many times over the years. This is the 10th year since Randi's passing. I still cannot explain my selfish desire to tuck those emotions deep. I have not done well with it personally, and yet I feel guilty when I think of the degree of loss. Randi's life and death have and will always be an impact on my life. As long as I live, she will always be remembered.

Deb Donahue
Nancy's Best Friend

I never had the privilege of meeting Randi, but during the last 10 years I have felt a sense of connection to her through her mother – Nancy. In 2000, Nancy and I were appointed to the newly formed Cumberland County Commission for Women. Following Randi's murder in 2003, I reached out to Nancy, and as the executive director of the local domestic violence agency, I wanted to assist her in any way that I could.

Following the death of Randi, Nancy and I were asked by the Commission for Women to co-chair a summit regarding violence against women and children in Cumberland County. During the planning of this summit, Nancy and I developed a strong professional and a personal relationship.

Over the next several years, Nancy became a strong advocate and voice for victims of domestic violence. Her desire to assist others despite her personal pain is remarkable. I know that Randi would be proud of her mother. I know that I am. I feel honored that Nancy has asked for my assistance with the formation of Randi's House of Angels to honor her daughter.

Nancy continues to have a huge impact on the lives of victims of domestic violence. Now she will concentrate on working with children who have been exposed to or have been a victim of domestic violence. What a great legacy to her daughter.

Ed Marsico
District Attorney, Dauphin County, Pennsylvania

There are certain cases that stay with you, that impact you both personally and professionally. The senseless murder of Jen and Dave on Christmas morning by a coward is one of them. For me, as a district attorney, my satisfaction comes from being able to provide justice. In my world, suicide doesn't equal justice.

As a father, each Christmas that passes I can't help but remember the letter and cookies on the table that Jen and Dave left for Santa. They serve as a reminder of how important my family is to me.

I'm amazed, too, by the effect that their lives have had on thousands because of Lynn's efforts.

Deb (Friday) Salas
Disc Jockey who was Harassed and Stalked by Tom Snead

My life changed the moment I stepped outside my work-place one seemingly typical night and discovered my smashed windshield. I had never been the target of such hatred. Had the act intended to instill fear in my heart, the goal had been achieved. This was also the night that my idealistic view of law enforcement came crashing down, as an apathetic and careless officer disregarded my potential leads and concern.

That was the night I started looking back -- back to make sure no one was following. My awareness was heightened to an uncomfortable degree, as every stranger and car following me were potential threats. But my fear was not crippling. It forced a dependence on God that I had never experienced before as I cried out, "Lord, keep me safe, please protect me," and I took the necessary steps to feel more secure, including the transition from living alone to a town house with others. With family an hour away, I was blessed with a protective and helpful new friend and surrounded by caring co-workers who didn't minimize my situation.

The impact of this time and the subsequent deaths of Jennifer and David have been far-reaching. The call I received on Christmas Day 1994 triggered conflicting emotions. I was thankful that I was safe and that the threat posed to me had been removed. I was thankful that I wouldn't have to deal with a trial and satisfied with the knowledge that he would receive God's judgment. But my thankful heart was coupled with devastation and confusion regarding the deaths of such beautiful young children, and for years I wondered if I had done enough. Could I have done just one more thing that may have altered the events? But then my support system would step in, "You did all you could," and I would be temporarily released from my "what if" thoughts.

The situation impacted my life in my 30s as I shared the events with a man I was getting to know and falling in love with. It was important to me that my future spouse understood what I had gone through. Locking the house, being mindful of danger – that does not come naturally to everyone. The fact that this man was attentive to all those details, plus a counselor and a third-degree black belt, was a huge blessing.

When I was contacted about this book, I found myself reliving the events -- this time not as a young radio announcer, but as a mother of two young sons. It was the first time I processed the death of Lynn's children through the lens of a mother. I was overwhelmed with emotion and grieved in a way that I had not 18 years prior. And then the question was posed, did I want to meet Lynn? Prior to our meeting, feelings of doubt returned – had I done enough? Had Lynn been mad at me all these years? Did she want to hurt me? I also felt inferior after reading about all Lynn and Nancy had gone on to do to help others in the wake of their sorrow, and questioned whether I had missed the purpose of the event in my life.

Our meeting began with an embrace, eliminating all fear. Little did I know Lynn had read a news article years ago that expressed how much I had tried to do to call attention to Mr. Snead's instability, and she harbored no ill will against me.

On that day, those negative ripples ceased. Thankfully, the positive ripples of this experience will never cease. I believe a person can learn from and is changed by every trial -- I will continue to love more, take nothing for granted, empathize in ways others can't when in a similar situation, and be aware of how I may be able to help others in the future.

Ed Monk
Lynn's Father

Lynn's father is a World War II veteran, a tank driver who survived the Battle of the Bulge. But not even the horrors of war prepared him for the trauma of losing two grandchildren:

I can remember saying at the dinner table on Thanksgiving Day in 1994 how lucky we were as a family that we never had any tragedy or illness in our family. You think crime only happens to those on the news. Jennifer and David's murder was really hard on our entire family.

They were two good kids. The wife was really close to them. We spent a lot of time together. I had 65 acres, and I can remember one time when we loaded them in the Jeep and took them camping. We drove around the mountains for about half an hour and then found a site where we pitched tents and built a campfire and grilled hotdogs, cooked beans and later roasted marshmallows. Jen and Dave didn't know it, but we were only about 100 yards from the house. They had a great time.

Jen and Dave left us with a lot of great memories.

Ed Katz
Lynn's Co-worker

In September of 2000, I retired as chief of the Penbrook Police Department and began a new career with the Office of Victims' Services at the Pennsylvania Commission on Crime and Delinquency, working under Lynn's leadership.

On my second day of employment, Lynn scheduled a meeting for us to discuss restitution. I was mortified. I had never met a parent who had lost two children to homicide, and now I was going to be sitting face-to-face with her. I remember weighing every word that came out of my mouth. All I could think about was saying something wrong, something that would dredge up memories of her not-so-distant past.

Thirteen years have passed since that day. Working with Lynn, who brought Jen and Dave into the workplace, opened my eyes to look at crime and its impact in a different light. I'm no longer uncomfortable talking to victims about the crime or about the person who died. I understand the impact and embrace opportunities to become involved in work that will make a difference in the lives of children. Recently, I became a board member for Randi's House of Angels.

Shannon Wood
Jennifer's Best Friend

In 1994, I was 10 years old and Jennifer's best friend. We were two peas in a pod and always found something to get ourselves in to.

Prior to her death, I hadn't really experienced the loss of someone close, at least no one I had spent as much time with as I had Jen. Jen and Dave's deaths permanently scarred me. I no longer had a sense of security, even around my own family members. I hated being alone in the dark, and I actually asked my dad if he would ever do something like Tom did to Jen.

My dad and I are very close, and I recently talked with him about how he felt when I questioned him. He was caught off guard and had never expected me to think he would ever do such a thing. At 10 years old, your mind is capable of producing a variety of vivid images. I've often said that I should have gone to see a therapist or someone who could help me talk through my feelings. I held my fears and thoughts inside for so long and would break down over something small when I hit my boiling point. As time went on, I was able to deal with the loss of Jen and slowly moved forward.

Nineteen years later, and every so often I still relive the night that I found out Jen and Dave were killed, and the sequence of events is still fresh in my mind. I remember the sound of my older sister Mandie's voice when I answered the phone. She asked for my dad, whose immediate reaction was to take my mom and grandfather upstairs to tell them what Mandie had seen on the 11 o'clock news. I distinctly remember sprinting upstairs when I heard my mom break down and having my dad put his arm around my shoulder as a tear ran down his cheek. He told me that a terrible thing had happened and Jennifer and David had been killed that morning.

Surprisingly, my parents took me to their funeral so that I could say goodbye. I barely made it through that day and cried more tears than I ever thought imaginable. I am so thankful my family was there to support me.

I often see or hear things that trigger good memories that Jen and I made. I recently heard "Whoomp! (There it is)," a popular song by Tag Team from 1993. I immediately saw myself as a kid in overalls and a bandana singing karaoke with Jennifer. We knew that song by heart and would dance around, singing loud enough for the neighbors to hear.

I wonder what things would be like if this tragedy had never happened. I celebrated our graduation together and other milestones, and when I marry the one I love, a part of Jen will be with me as I walk down the aisle. I wish she was here in person to be a part of my life, but am so thankful for the time we had together (from the time we were two years old until her death) and the positive impact she had on my life, whether she knew it or not.

I've made it a personal goal to help children who have experienced death as a result of domestic violence. In 1994, there weren't many support groups for children who were dealing with the death of a friend. I am now working on this goal as a board member with Randi's House of Angels. I make it a point to remind my peers that domestic violence does not only affect immediate family members. It can negatively impact the friends of children involved. I can only hope that I am able to change a child's life and help them cope and deal with death in a more positive way.

Kathy Wilson
A Friend of Paul's at the Time of Jen and Dave's Murder

Lynn found this letter on Jen and Dave's grave Christmas morning 1998:

December 24, 1998
Dear Jen and Dave,

Each and every day, you are remembered and missed by so many people who love you. The pain of losing you continues to be felt by an incredible number of people – especially your mom, and most especially at this difficult time of the year.

I want you to know that you are not forgotten. I want you to know that we are thankful for the continuing gift of your spirits, as thoughts of you continue to bless us and still warm our hearts and make us smile. I want you to know that your lives here were not in vain.

This world of ours is filled with many injustices in our daily struggles in life, and our quest to make sense of it all oftentimes goes unanswered.

I suppose there is a reason why God needs young angels, too, although that is something we will never understand while we are still here on earth. I know that one day, when we are once again with you, we will then be able to understand the reasons for why some things happen.

But until that time, please continue to watch over your mom and provide comfort to her. I know how proud you must be of the wonderful, loving, exceptional person that she is! Each and every day, her heart is filled with pain, and yet she continues on and accomplishes so many great things to help others in need.

Sending you love on this and every day...

Kathy

(Kathy, a friend of Paul's and a stranger to Lynn at the time of Jen and Dave's murders, was struggling with their deaths and

could not get their mother out of her mind. Early in 1995, Paul introduced Kathy to Lynn, and an amazing friendship developed. Kathy was one of the friends who helped Lynn through the "tougher years" and surrounded her with love.)

The death of Jen and Dave has taught me that anyone, anywhere, can be a victim of domestic violence. No one is immune. And I always tell people that from that day on, it became my barometer by which to measure if I am really having a bad day or not. It doesn't take long to realize that I'm not.

And, importantly, it made me very aware that it's important to simply be there for someone who is going through such a traumatic event. Don't try to tell them you know how they feel; don't try to (stupidly) suggest they "get over it"; don't hesitate to mention their loved one's name. Realize that memories can bring joy. One of the worst things you can do is to act as if the loved one never existed. And don't worry so much about what to say, just be there for them!

Pastor Pat Wirick
Lynn's Minister

With all that Lynn has been through, the most remarkable thing to me is what such a soft-spoken, gentle person has done with her grief and loss. While being a part of Lynn's journey over the past 19 years, she has taught me to see things through a different lens. This experience has taught me to be more open to life lessons. They can come from the most unexpected places. The first time I met Lynn she was deciding whether or not to fight for her life. She is very much one of the saints in my life, one of the people who lives the faith.

Because of Jen and Dave's deaths, I have learned to be more aware and mindful in several ways. It was obvious Tom had some mental health issues, but it was unimaginable that they could lead to such tragedy. As people started to put the pieces together to try to understand what had happened, it became clear there were a lot of little things that when taken alone would be seen as having little consequence, but when put together revealed a glimpse of an unstable person. Knowing how badly things can end has led to paying a lot more attention to where things are and where they might lead, and in some instances in being more proactive than I would like to be.

There is no way to escape the horror that is part of Jen and Dave's story, but it is not their whole story. I have learned that memories should not be silenced or avoided because of an inability to separate how alive they were from how they died. Nor is it right to try to "protect" Lynn from the pain of remembering or talking about Jen and Dave by avoiding or trying to move conversations away from talking about children or parenting. It deprives her of one of the greatest joys of parenthood: talking about her kids.

Finally, God speaks to us and through us and touches our lives in more ways than we might ever imagine. The expressions of love, care and concern, the friendship and prayers, the hugs and the food, the words of comfort and hope, all these things are examples of God's presence in Lynn's life at an incredible time of need. That she received them is a blessing. What she did with them is what makes her one of my saints.

She went to prison and asked prisoners to think of their victims, she went to the victims and told them of the freedom to forgive, she went to seminary to help show ministers how to minister, she worked for legislative changes to help protect children, she has worked for victims in more ways than one can count, and in all places she asks all of us to look within and find our true humanity, to find the image of God that is in us all, and to let this be what guides us to a different kind of wholeness.

Leo and Ruthie Brown
(Jen and Dave's Second Set of Parents)

Since losing Dave and Jen, we are watchful of abuse that may be happening to children and are not silent, even if it offends a parent. In general, we are very sensitive to abuse, whether it involves a child or an adult. As time went on and our anger towards Tom faded, we realized how naïve we were about mental illness. Afterwards, we could look back and see the signs, but as they were happening, we didn't recognize the signs of his mental illness. We were never exposed or knew much about mental illness.

We have spent many days and nights with Lynnie talking about and remembering Jen and Dave. We have talked about the good times and the special memories we have of them. We also have spent many days and nights crying together and trying to put our lives into proper perspective. Lynn always thanked us for listening when she needed to talk, but she doesn't realize how much she has helped us by just being herself. We can see Jen and Dave in her smile, in her laugh and in her mannerisms. Dave and Jen's spirit lives in and through her.

Paul Shiner
Lynn's Husband

Until December 25, 1994, I had only witnessed death up close once. My father died in 1988 after fighting heart disease for many years. But this time death was unexpected, violent, and shocking. So much so, that as I experienced it, beginning with finding Jen and Dave dead in their beds, it was as if I was having another person's nightmare. Yet, my experience was just a small gust of wind to what was Lynn's tsunami. Never have I seen a human being as emotionally devastated as Lynn was that Christmas morning. Although never attempted, suicide was a real option for Lynn.

The early years were Lynn's most difficult. With support and love from friends and family and a belief in eternal life, she somehow survived. But it was her altruism that gave her reason to live. Given the opportunity to work in victims' services by the state of Pennsylvania and through her varied initiatives in the private sector, Lynn has dedicated herself to the welfare of all victims. I know that this is her way of honoring her slain children, believing that they will be proud when they reunite forever.

The tragedy of Jen and Dave to me was liked getting splashed in the face with a bucket of cold water while sleeping. Since waking up, much has changed. Money was always the most important thing. Now it is time spent with loved ones. I've never been suspicious of a person's motives, but now I know one never really knows what is in another person's mind. And most importantly, I never really loved anyone except my child until Lynn. Ironically, through tragedy, we have formed a bond of unconditional love based on respect and trust that can never be broken. With every new day, I continue to do everything within my means to help Lynn reach others. That is my gift to Jen and Dave.

Chapter 14

Lynn's Closing Thoughts...

Christmas Day 2013 will be 19 years since the deaths of my babies. Yes, they will always be my babies. I will always carry a sadness and longing for them. As you have witnessed by sharing in my journey, I've worked hard to make a life without my children. I've fallen and gotten back up many, many times and am proud that I now can embrace each day by asking how I can make a difference in someone else's life. It's sort of simple. All one has to do is open her eyes and heart. While on this earth, it's my small gift to my children.

My message to each of you, with love, Lynn

To Jen and Dave:

Jennifer, when you smiled, it made my heart smile. David, when you smiled, it made my eyebrows rise, wondering what you were up to next. You have left me with many beautiful memories that have helped me in my darkest times.

Jen, I remember…

How proud you were to have a baby brother and how well you took care of him, wrapping David as well as all of your other babies in blankets and lining them up on the living room floor.

The notes I would find under my pillow, in my coat pocket or in my lunch bag telling me in different ways how much you loved me.

Going to your softball games, and you were in the infield doing cartwheels on the baseline as the batter was swinging at the ball.

How you made up menus for David and me to select what we would like to "order" for dinner. You then would make and serve us the dinner and leave a bill next to our plates.

David, I remember…

How you would help me unload the groceries from the car and days later I would find ice cream, cookies and other snacks stored in the back of your closet.

How proud I was of you when you introduced me to your friend at a school event. You told me later the kids in your class weren't always nice to him and he needed a friend. (The child had a developmental disability.)

You didn't like me jogging by myself, so you would ride your bike beside me when you could have been playing with your friends.

I remember how good you were at baseball and you being the youngest pitcher on the team. Each time you would bring the glove up to your face, you would look over at me and I could tell you were smiling behind the glove as you got ready to throw the ball.

I also remember…

The smiles on your faces when you gave me a bouquet of flowers for Mother's Day and there were bulbs attached. (They came from the neighbor's yard.)

How your faces lit up when we went to Disney World and Mickey and Minnie walked up to you to shake your hands.

The fun we had playing Wiffle Ball in the backyard, and how much you loved it when your cousins Bobby and Leigh Ann would babysit you.

I believe that you have been with me and continue to provide me with strength each and every day, helping me through all the different directions of my journey. Your presence in my life has been a blessing, and my life will be complete when you are in my arms.

To a Parent Who Has Lost a Child:
I'm sorry for your loss.

Remember, time does not heal. What time will do is allow you to learn how to cope with the tragedy and find a way to weave it into your new life. Honestly, it is the hardest thing you will ever go through. Honor your loss, yourself, where you have been, where you are and where you are headed. Be gentle and kind to yourself. Take it minute by minute, hour by hour or day by day. Surround yourself with loving, supportive and caring individuals. If that doesn't describe your inner circle, remove them. Trust me, you don't need any additional challenges.

In accepting the death of your child, over time you will come to an understanding that you cannot control all of the events in your life. Nor, in some cases, can you change them. You may also gain a wisdom that feels beyond your years. You may have an epiphany, truly understanding and valuing the importance of life and always making time for those who care about you. We've learned the hard way how precious life is. Embrace it.

For those moms whose child has been murdered, you will always be your child's mother. Your love is forever. The connection between a mom and a child is like no other. The loss of your child will never fade away until your heart stops beating and you take your last breath.

To Those Who Inspire Me:

Many people on the outside looking in ask those who choose to work in the field of victim services why they would want to work with so much pain, anger, grief, anguish?

The answer is always the same: to be able to help someone whose life has been forever changed. They watch them go into the blackest hole imaginable and then slowly, ever so slowly, transcend. Their pain, anguish and hopelessness is often incomprehensible. These victims don't feel courageous or strong, but advocates watch them take steps every day that they can't imagine being able to take themselves. Often times, they label victims as courageous and strong. Advocates know and hear that victims don't feel it, but it is what they feel about them. Crime victims inspire advocates. Crime victims and advocates inspire me. I know firsthand that advocates are truly touched by the physical and emotional harm endured by victims as a result of crime, but they are also grateful that victims reach out to them and allow them to be a part of their extraordinary journey.

Advocates come to us in many ways. Not only are they the professionals who dedicate their lives to helping victims of crime, they are also our family members, friends, co-workers and many other professionals who help us to cope with the victimization that we have suffered and endured at the hands of another and move forward in our lives.

I cannot begin to adequately express the importance of advocates. I know without a doubt I wouldn't be where I am today without them.

Their ability to touch victims' lives, to listen, to be comfortable in the silence, to guide, to support, to simply be there during some of the worst moments of their lives is profound. The devastation, grief, pain. … Advocates can't imagine stepping into their shoes … but they are willing to walk beside them, share their tears, validate their feelings and simply be. That is a blessing beyond words.

I am but one single voice among many. But let me say, never ever doubt the value and incredible difference advocates make in the lives of victims.

To all of the advocates and crime victims who have touched my life, you have left a profound imprint on my soul. Your love, support, friendship and guidance has lifted and carried my saddened spirit when I needed it most. You continue to inspire me to want to make a difference. The definition of inspiration is "divine guidance or influence exerted directly on the mind and soul of humankind." That is a definition that suits each of you. I'm forever grateful.

To Nancy Chavez:

While you are also one of the advocates who inspire me, I want you to know that it has been an honor to write this book with you. Sharing our deepest thoughts, fears, memories, tears and laughter has helped me to grow as a person. In the years to come, I'm certain that the sharing of our story with others will have become a critical part of our journey. I'm also certain that Randi is incredibly proud of her mother. I'm blessed to have you in my life.

To my Number One Advocate, Paul:

We've only been together 20 short years. Our relationship is one of a kind in my eyes. Your selfless commitment, unconditional love, compassion and constant support is a huge part of who I am today. You complete me. This book is a tribute to all we have done together to make a difference in the lives of others. You mean the world to me, and I honestly don't know where I'd be today without you. You are my rock and an amazing source of strength. Every morning that I wake up and feel you beside me, I still pinch myself and ask what I ever did to deserve someone like you in my life. Here's to another 30 baby.

Chapter 15

Nancy's Closing Thoughts...

Like many things in my life, I had a plan for my golden years. I planned to grow old with my daughter Randi and her family, waiting for her call so I could babysit my grandchildren. I thought of the places I would take them and the games we would play together. I envisioned a house filled with laughter and happiness on holidays and Sundays.

Although simple, that dream will never happen. Never will I hear the laughter of my grandchildren echoing through my home. Never will I see my beautiful daughter again. Randi is gone. I will never get her back.

When tragedy strikes our lives, we can be knocked off balance and bruised by the fall. Some may heal overnight; others require a lifetime to heal. We all take some part of the pain to our graves.

Ever since Randi was murdered, I have searched for her. I've looked for a special place where I could sit, close my eyes and remember a time when I was happy, when she was happy. At first, I could not think of going into Randi's room alone. I would stand at the doorway and hold onto the door frame. I did that many times until I had the courage to step into her world. I would caress her favorite stuffed toys, read the inscription on her school awards, run my fingertips across the dresses that hang in her closest in the hopes of staying close to her. There were times when I would climb into her bed to try to imagine once again the softness of her hands, the sound of her voice and the smile in her eyes. Now I walk past her room and smile because I know there is a place where Randi and I can be together.

It's been 10 years since I lost my little girl, and each day I try to recall a different memory of our years together. Sometimes I get scared because I think I won't be able to remember her. I won't lie, there have been some rocky places along my path to healing, but as I move forward, I have become stronger. There were times when I wanted it all to end. I would sit at the edge of my bed for hours or look at myself in the bathroom mirror until I no longer recognized the face staring back at me.

But I have learned over the past 10 years that some things happen for a reason. I have gained information and fortitude going through things that I never imagined. I know my problems now are less difficult. I know that God never gives you more than you can handle. I had to do this on my own terms. I know now that I needed to save my life in order to move forward. Perhaps after you read my story, you will understand why it is a story of hope, promise and survival. My story is like those told by survivors throughout the world.

What I know now is that one of life's most precious gifts is having family and friends who love you and trust you enough to share the pain they feel. Without a doubt, this book was not written without my family and friends, who have allowed me to lean on them for support, friendship, love and comfort.

My closest friends supported me as I ventured on a new path to fill the void in my life created by the loss of Randi. They gave me that extra push and reminded me that I was doing the right thing. They gave me hope and courage and taught me how to accept a gift with generosity of spirit. I believe the greatest gift is that we found each other.

I have a new journey in life now. I understand that living my life to its fullest means being prepared to capture the opportunity of each moment and to recognize all the possibilities. Through Randi's House of Angels, I am inspired to help children who are exposed to and may be victims of domestic violence. We cannot disregard that all children need our attention, our caring and our love -- the same love as I gave to my daughter – without selfishness or anger. No one should be allowed to take that from them.

Perhaps my life would have been different if Randi had lived. But I am a changed woman and there is no going back. I have realized that my life has not ended in spite of what happened. Little by little I began to accept the circumstances, to adjust to them, and make the most of them. I will never get over my sorrows, but I continue to move ahead.

My only wish is that I could stand beside all the mothers who find themselves standing at their child's grave site, trying to recapture the happiness, the love and the memories. I want to stand with the mothers who wrap themselves in their child's clothing trying to recapture the smell of her perfume or his cologne.

Just remember, you are never alone. Time does heal.

Organizations and Resources

The following is a list of sources of information that have been found to be helpful to survivors of homicide victims and those who serve them. This list is not intended to be comprehensive.

PA Crime Victims Website www.pacrimevictims.com
The website provides information on trauma and healing, how to follow an offender through the criminal and juvenile justice system, rights and services available to crime victims statewide and in specific counties and how to obtain financial help and free counseling. Crime victims also can learn how to sign up for notification when perpetrators are released from prison. If you are outside of Pennsylvania, call your district attorney's office or the office of the chief prosecutor in your county and ask if they have the services that you are seeking. If they do not, request a referral to a program in your area.

Gift from Within is a non-profit organization dedicated to those who suffer post-traumatic stress disorder (PTSD), those at risk for PTSD, and those who care for traumatized individuals. **www.giftfromwithin.org**

If you or a loved one has been affected by a drunk or drugged driving crash, **Mothers Against Drunk Driving (MADD)** is available to help. **www.madd.org**

Parents of Murdered Children (POMC) is an organization that provides support and assistance to all survivors of homicide victims. **www.pomc.com**

The Compassionate Friends is an organization that supports bereaved families grieving the death of a child of any age, from any cause. **www.compassionatefriends.org**

U.S. Department of Justice, Office for Victims of Crime, offers a national clearinghouse of information for crime victims and victim advocates. **www.crimevictims.gov**

National Center for Victims of Crime is a leading resource and advocacy organization for crime victims and those who serve them. **www.victimsofcrime.org**

National Alliance on Mental Illness (NAMI) is an organization dedicated to building better lives for the millions of Americans affected by mental illness. **www.nami.org**

The Dart Center for Journalism and Trauma is dedicated to informed, effective and ethical news reporting on violence, conflict and tragedy. The Center's website provides timely articles, expert interviews, journalist-to-journalist advice, and other resources. **www.dartcenter.org**